CRASH COURSE

on
Successful Parenting

13
DYNAMICS
OF
RAISING
GREAT
KIDS

A Division of Thomas Nelson Publishers
Since 1798

www.thomasnelson.com

Published by J. Countryman ® a division of Thomas Nelson, Inc., Nashville, Tennessee 37214

Written by Jessica Inman

www.jcountryman.com
www.thomasnelson.com

Designed by Randall Miller Design, Tulsa, Oklahoma

ISBN 1-4041-8657-3

Printed in China

CRASH COURSE

on
Successful Parenting

13
DYNAMICS
OF
RAISING
GREAT
KIDS

Table of Contents

Introduction

To the Reader:

Think with me for a moment about someone you know who has already raised some wonderful children. Get them in mind. Most likely you see smiling faces, cooperation, and love. Family fun times followed by children entering adulthood poised for success rounds out the picture.

When you talk with these parents, they all say the same thing; "We are so blessed!" Oh, yes, it is an absolute blessing to have a happy family resulting in successful children. But make no mistake, it does not happen by accident. Luck plays no part in raising wonderful children, either.

Knowledge, forethought, and love forged into good parenting skills carried out on a daily basis are what it takes to raise great children. Unfortunately, most parenting decisions are made on the spur of the moment and motivated by emotional extremes. This is too bad for both the parents and the children. Trial-and-error parenting often produces family chaos and less than successful children.

Think of it this way. Suppose you were going to build a house. What is the first thing you would do? If you could not hire someone to do it for you, you would have to get a lot of training in building skills if you were to have any hope of ending up with a well-built house. If you are like most, you neither have the money nor desire to have someone raise your children. This leaves you with two choices. You can either get the training you will need to raise your children, or you can go with the trial and error approach.

Since you have read this far, the approach you prefer is obvious. Knowing you're ready for the task of learning, the challenge becomes one of time—where do you get the time to learn about parenting when all of your time is taken up by parenting? Well, that's what the Crash Course books are all about: giving you the essential information needed in a format that you can quickly access.

So, welcome to a crash course on successful parenting. It is a great book filled with loads of useful information. Best of all, the information is segmented to apply to all age categories of children, from babies to teens.

Happy Parenting!

Larry J. Koenig, Ph.D.
Series Consultant and General Editor

P.S. This is an expertly written book on every important parenting topic imaginable. Enjoy!

CHAPTER 1

The Four Things Your Kids Need Most

---

*The home should be a warm sanctuary
from the storms of life for each member
of the family. A haven of love and acceptance.
Not only children, but also parents,
need this security.*

—ANONYMOUS

POWER STATEMENT:

Master the parenting
"biggies," and everything
else will fall into place.

Parenting might be broken down into "macro parenting" and "micro parenting." There are big-picture goals we set for ourselves, like giving our kids a sense of responsibility and respect for others, and then there are the smaller goals, like getting them to school on time. As it happens, the macro and the micro issues of parenting are inseparable—we meet our macro goals by setting and meeting micro goals.

Here are the four "biggies"—your kids' greatest needs—and a few practical ideas on meeting them in the middle of everyday life.

Macro Goal: Love

What your kids need most may not seem so difficult: love. You already love your kids so much it's sometimes frightening. So how do you make sure they know it?

Kids need to feel overwhelmingly accepted, to know that there's nothing they could do to make you not want to have a relationship with them anymore. The only way to go about giving them that sense of security is to be proactive in nurturing a relationship with them—spending time with them and intentionally taking an interest in them and their lives.

Sometimes when we're worried about making sure our kids feel loved, the temptation arises to avoid conflict or discipline, thinking our exchanges with our kids must always be happy in order to be loving. But the truth is that when discipline is done for the good of a child (not to relieve our own anger and frustration), it is one of the strongest expressions of love. Good parental love focuses on a kid's needs and well-being, not necessarily their wants or our frustrations.

Is it possible to love our kids too much? In a word, no. However, it is possible to praise our kids too much, making them dependent upon praise or paving the way for perfectionistic tendencies later in life. It's also possible to foster such an emotional closeness with a child that he or she becomes "adultized," more of a confidant and friend than a son or daughter, which can cause a child feelings of insecurity, as well as disrupt family life if the child receives an elevated status over her siblings or even your spouse. Plus, it sets the child up for a painful "dethronement" process in the classroom when she doesn't get the special treatment she's used to at home.[1]

A few micro goals for showing love include:

- Nip power struggles in the bud by setting sensible limits and sticking to them. Limits nurture a child's sense of loving security— and minimize those exasperated moments where you lose your cool and wonder whether you even like your kid.

- Make sure your kids get some affection from you every day—a note in a lunch box, a hug, an "I love you."

- Over dinner tonight, do some active listening. Ask questions, make eye contact, and don't interrupt until your kids are finished talking. Listening is a great way to say "I love you."

- Avoid making comparisons between your kids, banishing phrases like, "Why can't you be more like your sister?" from your vocabulary.

Macro Goal: Time

One of the best ways to show love to your kids is to give them your time. Time is priceless as an expression of love—and as an avenue for your other parenting goals.

Time is the glue that holds family life together. It's hard to know what your kids are facing in school, for example, without a little focused time each day. Plus, there is simply no substitute for your presence. Lawrence E. Shapiro states that a parent's physical presence is a huge factor in a child's ability to overcome the psychological effects of a trauma.[2] But kids don't have to be in the middle of a crisis to need their parents' presence and love.

And there is no point in your kids' lives in which they need your time less than others. Even as your teens depend on you less and less, they still need time with you to hash out the difficulties of life, to try ideas out on you, or if nothing else, simply to know that you're available when they do need some advice.

And yet time is an issue very conducive to guilt for many of us. A horde of tasks and activities clamors for our time, and we just don't spend as much time with our kids as we'd like. But as easy as it is to give in to guilt, it's better to shake off our guilty feelings and simply resolve to make spending time with our kids a top priority—guilt-ridden parenting tends to lose its joy and objectivity, which is never good for kids. Plus, the real value of time spent with kids has to do with focused attention, not necessarily with duration. (In other words, while quantity is important, it's not as important as quality.)

Here are some micro goals for giving kids your time:

- If you're feeling a little stretched out, spend a little time evaluating your activities. Have you overcommitted yourself? In what area can you pare back a little?

- Maximize the time you have with your kids by doing some multitasking. Make cooking dinner a family activity, or turn off the radio in the car so you can talk to your kids.

- Implement a standing "date" with each of your kids. It doesn't have to be a big production—just a little space of time dedicated to just the two of you. Take a fifteen-minute walk every night after dinner, or play a card game just before bedtime.

- Ever think about a monthly family meeting? Try it this month: Sit everyone down to talk about recent events and encourage your kids to bring up anything that's bothering them.

CASE STUDY:

One father solved the problem of spending quality time with his kids through something as simple as Ping-Pong.

"I was always trying to get my teen son to talk with me about the big issues in his life. The more I pushed, the more he withdrew and withheld. He just wasn't going to open up with me. I ended up frustrated and mad. I'm sure he felt the same way.

"I finally stopped pushing. He likes to play Ping-Pong; I like Ping-Pong. So we started playing every night. We've gotten pretty close, and we've actually had some great conversations. I finally figured out he just needed time, and the quality part of time couldn't be forced."

Macro Goal: Consistency

It's hard to overstate the need for consistency. Consistency makes daily family life seem infinitely easier and is the key to successful discipline. Plus, consistency makes a child feel safe and gives them greater confidence in you as a trustworthy authority figure—and that trust is priceless.

Being consistent means doing what you say you'll do, following through on promises and discipline. It means setting reasonable (and flexible) house rules and sticking with them. It means not making flash decisions based on momentary emotions.

It's also good to have some consistency of routine, doing more or less the same things at more or less the same time each day. Consistent routines give kids a sense of stability and offer an opportunity to develop independence and self-esteem as kids learn to perform daily tasks with minimal prompting.

But establishing consistency is easier said than done, of course, especially on those afternoons where the dishwasher is leaking, the dog won't stop barking at the FedEx guy, you just found out that your oldest has a science fair project due tomorrow, and all your youngest wants is to eat an ice cream bar fifteen minutes before dinner, just this once. *Please?* And while there's no need to be an ice cream Nazi just for the sake of rule-keeping, when you're frustrated and tired, it's just as easy to be inconsistent in the non-negotiables as in the negotiables.

Exasperation is the enemy of consistency. And the best way to stave off exasperation is to have a plan. Set up a routine. Have a set of guidelines regarding TV, going over to friends' houses, meals, and how to treat other family members that will help your kids know what to expect. And know in advance what's negotiable and non-negotiable; as a rule, health and safety issues and treating others with respect should always be non-negotiable.

But don't think consistency means holding rigidly to rules and ignoring special circumstances. Nancy Samalin and Catherine Whitney write that sometimes you may decide to bend a house rule for a particular reason, and that's okay.

SIX HOUSE RULES

The key to house rules is to discuss them, post them, and explain them. Here are six suggestions you might incorporate into your own family's list of rules.

- No hitting, kicking, or name-calling. Treat family members and guests with respect.

- If you make a mess, clean it up. Leave each room the way you found it.

- If you borrow something, ask first. Return it in good condition.

- Do all the chores assigned to you by Mom or Dad.

- Do all your homework.

- Ask permission before going to a friend's house or having a friend over.

Just make sure you explain the special circumstances surrounding your rule-bending by saying something like, "Tonight we're going to relax our rule about no TV before bedtime because there is a special on chimpanzees that I think we would all enjoy watching."[3]

Some micro goals for achieving consistency:

- Evaluate your consistency as you interact with your kids this week. When you say no, does it mean no? Or do your kids know they can get you to say yes if they press just the right button?

- Get a dry-erase board for the kitchen and write out the family's schedule, as detailed as "naptime" and "snack time" for your preschoolers. This will help you get everything into the day that you want, and it will help your kids get a sense of structure in their day and purpose behind their activities.

- Hold (another) family meeting this week to discuss your house rules. Get your kids' input and decide what your family guide-lines for behavior should be (and obviously, Mom and Dad have the final say). Write them out and post them on the refrigerator or a bulletin board. Explain your system of discipline—the first infraction gets a warning, the second gets a time-out, etc.— and be sure to stick with it!

Macro Goal: Security

The world is so big and scary to small children—and to most adults at least some of the time—and they need to know that their home is a safe place. Giving your kids loads of love, time, and attention and being consistent will go a long way toward meeting your kids' need for security. But there are other keys to security as well—

- Kids feel secure when they know they have a support network in place—friends and extended family who spend time with them and generally offer support to the family. It takes time to build that kind of network, and it may not be immediately possible to create strong bonds with some members of your extended family. Plus, you have to choose your support network carefully and guard your kids' influences. But there are options: Parenting support groups can be found in lots of churches and communities, and even a few close friends will add to your kids' sense of support.

- Change is hard for everyone to some degree or another, and children in particular need a little help making transitions. If you know a big change is coming for your family, prepare your kids by telling them what is about to happen and what they can expect.

- Watch your words. We cover the power of words in Chapter 3—what you say to and in front of your kids can affect their sense of

security in profound ways. Shield them
from the kind of arguments that might make
them worry about the state of the family and
be careful to encourage them.

Of course, there's a difference between security and
inflexibility. A rigidly fixed environment doesn't help a
child adapt to changes beyond your control. So it's
important to give kids challenges and responsibilities and
let them experience the consequences of their decisions,
especially as they leave their toddler years and begin
exploring the world more and more. And by exposing
them to different experiences while maintaining your
position as their ally and supporter, you give them an even
greater sense of stability.

Here are some micro goals for building your children's
sense of security:

- Build your parenting support group by
  calling a friend for a playdate with your
  kids or spending the day at Grandma's.
  If you're introducing new friends, be sure
  to go slow—give your kids time to get used
  to these new people, and don't expect them
  to spend long stretches of time with new
  friends immediately.

- Keep an eye on your words this week.
  Do you speak harshly to your spouse?
  Do you sharply criticize your kids? Do
  you appropriately handle your anger?
  Determine the areas you need the most

work on, and why you think you react the way you do in certain situations. Most of all, make an effort to speak positively to your family for a full week and see how it affects the climate in your home.

If you find yourself worrying about what your kids need and how to give it to them, remember that what your kids need most is a loving presence in their lives—and you're probably already there.

PERSONAL REFLECTION:

How would you describe the overall climate in your house? Would you say it's a safe place for your kids—do they feel loved and supported? What do you think could be improved? What are your family's strengths?

✓ *YOUR TO DO LIST:*

Tonight, turn off the TV and play a board game or bake some cookies. When it's time for bed, read an extra-long story and be sure to give your kids a hug when you say goodnight.

FOR FURTHER STUDY:

Loving Without Spoiling
    —by Nancy Samalin and Catherine Whitney

CHAPTER 2

Understanding Your Child

It is a wise father that knows his own child.

—WILLIAM SHAKESPEARE

POWER STATEMENT:

Successful parenting is informed parenting; we do what's best for our kids when we tailor our parenting to fit their needs.

It's not good to dwell on past mistakes, or the possibility of future mistakes. But it is good to make efforts to avoid mistakes. And the easiest way to make a mistake is to parent without considering our children's individual needs.

Sometimes we forget how hard it is to be a child. All kinds of confusing things happen during the growing-up process, and our kids can't always communicate what's going on in their hearts and minds. So while we can never expect to understand absolutely everything about our kids, we do need to tread carefully and seek to understand where our kids' behaviors are coming from as much as possible.

Dialogue is key—we understand our kids best by keeping open lines of communication with them. And as we listen and learn, it's also important to read between the lines, looking for the things our kids wouldn't necessarily know to tell us, like temperament and age-specific issues, and act accordingly. Understanding your child is mostly about understanding where they are in terms of develop-ment (how they're like lots of other kids) and their temperament (how they're like a smaller section of kids).

Stages of Development

The best step you can take toward understanding your child is to understand where most kids their age are in terms of development. No two kids are quite alike or follow the exact same path toward adulthood, but if you can grasp some of the developmental distinctives of each age, you've come a long way toward understanding your children's behavior and needs.

The First Year

Your baby is hard at work. Even when she's just sleeping or eating or playing, she's busily learning about the world, building muscles and bones, or creating new neural pathways. And while a lot of personality traits are evident from birth, your baby is highly receptive and moldable in his first year, and it's now that you lay the groundwork for his ability to trust and succeed.

What your baby needs most from you is a sense of security as he begins to explore the world. Be available and consistent. And interact with your baby throughout the day—talking, singing, and making eye contact—which will help speed along her language skills and brain development. The goal in parenting a baby is to let her know that you're trustworthy and to facilitate her mental, social, and physical development.

Toddlerhood

As your child keeps growing and begins walking, she's feeling ready for more independence, wanting to do things for herself and often imitating things she sees adults doing. A couple other key features of the toddler years include a short attention span (sometimes a very short attention span) and a fair degree of self-centeredness. Kids leave behind the egocentricity of babyhood and become more aware of others as they approach three years old.

As you parent a toddler, keep in mind their burgeoning independence. Give them opportunities to try new things, and as often as possible, don't do for them what they can do for themselves. A great way to lubricate life with your toddler is to give them choices: "Do you want peas or celery?" Choices nurture a toddler's sense of independence and will help you deal with the contrariness endemic to this age.

Discipline is important during the toddler years as you help your child develop self-control, but it's really important to take into consideration what your toddler is capable of obeying. It's not realistic, for example, to expect a toddler to sit absolutely still through a lengthy meeting or church service.

Key thought for the toddler years: They're gaining new levels of autonomy and starting to master their world—but they're still not little adults and shouldn't be treated as such.

Early School Age

Children's curiosity about the world around them continues to expand as they enter the school years. Kids this age love and need to test their boundaries, exploring their world and pushing their physical and mental capabilities. It's now that their self-esteem is best developed by trying and conquering new things.

You can help fulfill your children's curiosity by watchfully allowing them to explore their environment— walking with them to the end of the street, encouraging them to try the highest safe level of monkey bars—and helping them discover new interests. And kids this age love to help and be involved, so look for ways to incorporate them in your daily tasks and activities.

Socialization is very important now, as your kids are going off to school and becoming more social creatures, and they'll need you to facilitate their social lives and help them learn how to treat others.

Something else to consider about the early school years is that kids this age have active imaginations and may not have a complete grasp of reality—which means that when they tell stories, what appears to you to be a lie might just be the way they perceived the event they're discussing. So, just like during the toddler years, be careful about when and how you punish, keeping in mind your child's capabilities.

Late Grade School

At this age, kids are coasting toward puberty. They have

a stronger sense of identity than earlier in their lives—
they've accomplished a lot in the last few years—and
they haven't yet been thrown into the whirlwind of
adolescence. Now is a great time to play games and do
puzzles, to take advantage of the time you have before
clubs and sports start to crowd your lives.

This is a great age. Invest the time in getting to know
your kids now and building a relationship with them—
which will pay huge dividends when your kids hit
adolescence.

The Preteen Years

During the preteen years, kids are charging toward
adolescence in starts and stops—one minute your
daughter is experimenting with your makeup, the next
she wants to play Barbies with her little sister.

Now and in the coming years, a preteen's self-esteem
will take a beating, so they really still need their mommies
and daddies to hug them and love on them, no matter how
grown-up they may appear to be. And allow your preteen
those laid-back "kid" moments of playing on the swings
and calling you "Mommy." Those days pass all too soon, so
enjoy them now, and allow your kids to do so as well.

This can be a tough age in terms of energy level—boys
in particular tend to act up and be the class clowns in fifth
and sixth grade. It's usually just a normal excess of energy,

26

and it's pretty funny sometimes, but keep an eye on that kind of behavior and determine whether your preteen is acting up for some emotional or social reason. And, of course, they need to learn when to rein themselves in.

The Teen Years

As your preteen rounds the corner toward the early teen years, there are major changes ahead. Be prepared even for apparent changes in personality—young teens may become abrasive, mean, flighty, and tearful without a lot of warning or provocation. And be prepared to have your feelings hurt as you suddenly become the dumbest person alive in your kids' eyes. Try not to take it personally; as the adult, your job is to simply guide them through this rather confusing time.

Most teens share a sense that no one understands them. Their brains are simply undergoing a lot of changes, which has a way of distancing them from the rest of the world. The best way to comfort a teen who feels that no one understands him is to just acknowledge his feelings—"I'm sorry you're feeling so misunderstood"—rather than trying to convince him that he really is understood or that everyone his age feels that way.

As your teens get older, they'll have a lot more freedom, and a lot more choices, which can be downright scary. And sometimes teens feel like they're being harangued twenty-four hours a day, with adults on all sides telling them what not to do. While it's extremely important to talk to your kids about avoiding bad choices, the key to success lies in facilitating good choices, providing opportunities to discover their interests and forge their identities in healthy avenues.

The teen years are for letting go, slowly allowing your kids more and more independence and ending their dependence on you. And as tough and sad as that may sound, it comes with a great bonus: the joy of seeing who your child has become.

The Way They're Wired

As you attempt to understand your kids, their stages of development are a huge part of the equation, but there are other factors to consider as well. A big one is their personal makeup—the way their personality and temperament are "wired."

On a spectrum between "easy" and "difficult"—"easy" meaning adaptable, friendly, and obedient and "difficult" meaning cranky and resistant—most kids fall somewhere in the middle. If you have a kid who's on the difficult side, here are a few things to consider:

- Structure is going to be key in your fight for peace. Your more challenging child needs to know his boundaries and have them consistently enforced.

- Get out of the emotional blame game. It's not easy or fun to be the "problem" child in the family; you can cut the tension in your home and make her life better by choosing not to blame her or yourself for those difficult moments.

- Love, love, love. The best way to make life with your difficult child easier is to show him lots of love and affection.

On the other hand, if you have one of those "easy" children, there are a few reminders in order as well:

- With compliant kids, sometimes it's tempting to shelter them from the consequences of their actions or to skirt discipline just a little. After all, they try so hard to please and never seem to cause any problems. But while it's true we need to be careful with our sensitive kids, compliant children need discipline just as much as any other child.

- Easy kids' adaptable, go-with-the-flow nature leads to another temptation: Sometimes during tense family situations, it becomes tempting to slight an easy kid, knowing that they'll make less of a fuss than a difficult child if they don't get their way. Especially if you have a mix of easy and difficult children, you'll want to be careful to be fair.

Special Considerations

There are times when we have to look a little deeper

Everyone is different, and no one fits neatly into a preconceived personality formula. But looking at your kids' behaviors and traits is a great way to figure out how they view the world and how they need you to relate to them. John Trent and Kurt Osborne offer this model of categorizing personality traits that might help you determine where your child falls on the personality spectrum.

Lion

Lions take charge of everything they do, bossing their siblings and friends around—and sometimes even you! They're bold, assertive, decisive, and very competitive. A lion sets goals and drives forward until those goals are met.

Otter

Otter children are highly social and love to party. They're energetic, creative, and do well in groups. They're not very detail oriented, preferring instead to socialize. But they are big dreamers and good visionaries, and did we mention they love to party?

Golden Retriever

A golden retriever child is sunny, serene, and easy to get along with. Golden retrievers tend to go with the flow in family life and love to help others. They're very loyal and care deeply about people, which makes them prone to try to keep everyone happy.

Beaver

A beaver kid is one you have to pry away from his homework to make him come to dinner. Highly detail- and goal-oriented, beavers tend to get absorbed in tasks. They're also very deliberate, orderly, and analytical.

than their age or temperament to understand our kids' behavior, especially when their behavior is disrupting their lives. Kids who might appear to be lazy or underachieving may actually have a deeper problem.

As frightening and confusing as learning disabilities and emotional problems are for kids, they're often just as much so for parents. A child facing these kinds of hurdles needs parents who are his passionate advocates and informed consumers. Dr.

Larry B. Silver encourages parents to be those things for their learning-disabled children: "No one and no single agency—not your family physician, your child's teacher, the school, or anyone else—is as vitally concerned as you are, or as informed as you can and must be."[1] He goes on to offer more advice for parents of special needs kids:

- Educate yourself. It might be challenging to wade through all the material available, but your first step to helping your child is to learn everything you can about your child's condition—what causes it, how it's treated, and how you can help your child cope.

- Seek help. You can't depend solely on counselors and special education programs, but you don't have to do everything yourself, either. And if your school doesn't offer what you need, fight for your child, and do everything you can to get him what he needs.

- Don't overprotect. If you undershoot your child's capabilities and set your expectations too low, she'll conclude that she's incompetent and incapable of leading a normal life.

If you have a child with special needs, your ultimate goal is to nurture and encourage their strengths while helping them learn to overcome their weaknesses.

PERSONAL REFLECTION:

What do you think is the hardest thing about understanding your children? Do you think your parenting generally "hits" them where they are? Where do you think you need the most improvement?

✓ YOUR TO DO LIST:

Write up a profile for each of your children. On a separate notecard for each child, write their names, ages, and a few basic personality characteristics. What do you think are their greatest needs?

FOR FURTHER STUDY:

Personality Plus for Parents: Understanding What Makes Your Child Tick
—by Florence Littauer

www.zerotothree.org

CASE STUDY:

One of the things that Byron, a college athlete and all-around weekend warrior, most looked forward to as a parent was participating in sports with all of his kids, especially his boys. His second child and oldest boy, however, showed absolutely no inclination toward sports, and even experienced some physical barriers to athletic glory, including asthma and flat feet.

Byron did all the things an active, interested dad is supposed to do with his son—he threw a baseball and football in the backyard, coached youth soccer, took him to college and even professional ballgames. But as his son approached the teen years, Byron realized that his efforts were causing more conflict than companionship, and neither of them was having that much fun. So he made the decision to stop forcing athletics with his son and found other activities, including chess club and an annual automobile show in his town.

Is Byron disappointed? Yes and no. But mostly no, due to understanding that his son's interests were not only not identical to his own, but actually quite different.

The "Platinum Rule" states: Do unto others as they would have done unto them. That includes our kids.

The Power of Words

The words that a father speaks to his children in the privacy of home are not heard by the world, but, as in whispering-galleries, they are clearly heard at the end and by posterity.

—JEAN PAUL RICHTER

POWER STATEMENT:

Choose your words carefully: By what you say to your children, you have the power to equip them for life and success.

I t can't be overstated: How you talk to your child matters immensely. It's possibly the most important aspect of your parenting, and if you're not serious about watching your words, you're not serious about helping your children survive and thrive in the world. For one thing, your words can nurture your child, making them strong and confident in the face of challenges. For another thing, in order for your kids to become functioning members of society, they'll need to learn to communicate effectively, and they need you to model great communication for them.

If you're reading this book, you obviously want what's best for your kids. Allow us to offer you the Ten Commandments of Communication to guide you in speaking words that build up and help your child grow.

Thou Shalt Express Love to Thy Kids

Newsflash: Your kids need love.

Studies strongly link eating disorders with a lack of parental affection and acceptance. Sufferers of binge eating disorders, for example, "often do not experience being truly loved for themselves and have, in essence, given up on having empathic connections with people."[1] You are the first and foremost source of love and acceptance in your child's life.

Plus, all of your parenting goals hinge on your

relationship with your children—you can't teach them how to ride a bike or handle their money or manage stress unless they know you love them. And in order for them to know you love them, you have to tell them.

It's true that actions often weigh as much as words when it comes to expressing love. But there's simply no substitute for the words "I love you."

- Be consistent. Without being too automatic about it, don't let too much time go by without an "I love you."

- Be spontaneous. Make sure your kids know that you're not just saying you love them out of habit—they'll know you mean it when you say "I love you" spontaneously.

- Be strategic. Look for moments when your kids might be most receptive to an expression of love or when they might need it the most—a loss on the baseball field, a tough day at school, a moment of quiet in front of the TV.

Some of us have a tough time verbally expressing love. The words just don't flow effortlessly off our tongues—our parents didn't say it that often, or we just find the words a little intimidating. What matters most is that we make an effort to give our kids the affirmation they need.

Thou Shalt Often Point Out Thy Children's Strengths

The world is a harsh place. Particularly as your kids get older, all kinds of things conspire to make them question themselves and doubt their abilities and worth. That's why kids need their parents to be their allies and faithful fans.

The more you see your kids as valuable and important people and help them see themselves as such, the better their self-esteem will be. We'll talk more about self-esteem later, but for now, here are some things to consider:

- In order to be able to point out your kids' strengths, you have to know what they are. Look for the best in your kids—catch them being kind or funny; go to their athletic events; look over their schoolwork.

- If you're the kind of person who's especially hard on yourself, sometimes your self-criticism can bleed over into the way you talk to your kids, especially if you tend to worry about how their performance reflects on you. Resist that. For one thing, it's unfair to your kids. For another thing, it perpetuates a cycle of low self-esteem.

- If you're faithful in letting your kids know what you like about them, the next time you need to point out something they need to work on, you don't have to worry about it ruining their day—or week or month.

A word of caution: Another vital aspect of good communication is honesty. Your words of affirmation must be true to be effectual. If you tell a slow child who can't

CASE STUDY:

It was one of those situations that exhibit your parenting capabilities for the entire world to see: a few families out for a night of bowling. Jeannie and her teenage daughter Rebecca hung out at a table with another mom and daughter as others took their turns at the lanes. When the topic turned to kids' sports activities, Jeannie turned to Rebecca and said, "You sure never were very good at any sports. Well, I guess you did okay at gymnastics."

Rebecca didn't say a word. She just looked at the table and turned red.

Even if Jeannie had chosen to point out her daughter's athletic shortcomings in private rather than in front of other people, Rebecca could have done without her mother's observations, to say the least. And these casual, seemingly small encounters had regularly chipped away at her confidence for years— why would she try new activities knowing that if she failed, her mother would be sure to notice and comment? Kids hear a parent's words about their abilities more than anyone else's.

catch or throw that he's quick as a rabbit and great at football, he'll never believe another compliment from you again, and you'll end up digging a bigger hole for yourself than if you hadn't encouraged your child at all. Solution: Where you can't honestly affirm ability, affirm effort—"Son, I am so proud of you for working so hard every day at football practice. That kind of effort and persistence will pay off. Great job." (Obviously, if you can't honestly affirm effort or ability, don't affirm either!)

Thou Shalt (Correctly) Express Thy Anger

You may have noticed that sometimes your kids make you mad. They run into the street without checking for cars. They go to a friend's house without telling you where they're going. They use your vintage Willie Nelson albums as a track for their Hot Wheels.

When these kinds of things happen, think of them as an opportunity to model for your kids how to express anger without damaging the other person.

Anger is a thorny emotion. On one hand, you can't go through life never expressing your anger—it's bad for your health and cheats your kids out of learning to express emotion. On the other hand, there are times when we need to process our emotions before expressing them, and anger in particular needs to be treated with caution.

An improper expression of anger toward your kids

makes them feel as if your love and respect for them are in jeopardy: "I can't believe you would be so stupid" or "You'd better get your act together, or so help me…"

A proper expression of anger simply tells your child how you feel and why, then what you want him or her to do about it: "It made me so unbelievably furious when you shaved Mrs. Kleeman's cat. You're going over there to apologize first thing in the morning, and get ready for a long talk on respecting the feelings and property of other people."

To get a little self-control before you talk to the object of your anger, you might need to distance yourself from the situation a little. Take a walk. Work on the car. Shoot a few hoops. And try to remember that you did much worse things when you were their age.

Thou Shalt Listen Well

Part of the magic of words lies in what you *don't* say. Good listening is one of the most precious commodities in the parenting world. When you listen to your kids, you communicate to them that they're important to you—and you model an important life skill. Of course there's a time to teach and instruct your kids and give them advice. But great parents know the incredible power of listening.

Whether your four-year-old is telling you about a preschool field trip or your teenager has spontaneously decided to open an oasis of personal information, keep in mind the classic laws of listening:

- It's all about body language. As your child talks, turn your shoulders toward him or her and make eye contact. Sit upright and lean in.

- Show interest by nodding and using signifiers like: "Really?" "Uh-huh?" "And then what happened?"

- Listen to the whole story. Don't interrupt until you feel you understand what your son or daughter is trying to tell you. Resist the urge to dispense advice or solve the problem just yet—instead, try to identify their feelings: "It sounds like that made you sad."

If your son or daughter is describing a problem or hurt, the Supermom or Superdad in you will want to step in and fix things. But there's an art to allowing your children to think through the situation for themselves, and doing so will teach them valuable problem-solving skills.

To guide your child through the problem-solving process, start by asking a few questions, like, "Why do you think all this happened?" or "What do you think would be a good thing to do now?" Ask for more detail about their problem, and continue to listen intently as they elaborate. You'll probably find that your kids are savvier than you thought, and before too long, they'll probably have decided on a positive solution. With a loving parent as their sounding board, they can't go wrong.

Thou Shalt Explain

As important as it is to listen to your kids, it's also important to share information with them. There's a reason kids ask, "Why?" so often: They're constantly absorbing information about the world. When you patiently and kindly explain your decisions, you teach your kids and earn their respect. When you warmly share with your kids and make yourself available to help them sort through the information they receive, you make yourself their ally in figuring out the world around them.

A parenting style termed "authoritative," characterized by listening intently and explaining decisions to children, has been endorsed as conducive to raising self-reliant, cooperative, and explorative children. A few keys to parenting authoritatively include—

- Make decisions thoughtfully. There are times to rely on your instincts; but as often as possible, know why you're doing what you're doing and be able to explain it to your kids. When you declare the hour after dinner as a time strictly dedicated to home-work, make sure your kids know that you're doing so because part of being disciplined and working hard is devoting time to something.

- Ask questions: "Do you know why that policemen is giving that car a ticket?" Listen to her response, and visibly enjoy the ensuing conversation.

- Be careful not to be condescending. Yes, you're the parent, and yes, you may know more (though your kid probably often gives you a run for your money) but don't make your child feel as though he's incapable of understanding what you're saying.

Thou Shalt Talk

Your interactions are what cement your relationship with your kids, and your day is full of opportunities to bond—you just have to seize them. Proactively initiating and engaging your kids in conversation is the way to go. Here are some quick tips to get your kids to open up.

- Highlight common interests. Talk about your favorite shows or movies, sports, activities, or music. Look forward to upcoming events together. Buy mother-and-daughter or father-and-son copies of the same book to discuss.

- Ask questions that require more than a one-word response. Be sure to employ your listening skills when your child starts to answer.

- Set aside time. Some of your best interactions will be the ones that happen naturally and unintentionally, like a few minutes in the car on the way to softball practice, but it's also important to set aside time to interact. That family dinner everyone's always talking about isn't such a bad idea.

Thou Shalt Not Make Personal Criticisms

It's inevitable. You're going to have to correct your child, to point out something they need to do or not do or work to improve. But, as with anything, there's a right way and a wrong way to go about it. When you criticize your child, it's important that they know that you're taking issue with their behavior, not with them as a person.

If your son is having trouble staying organized, "Son, your school papers are too disorganized for you to work well" should never become "You're sloppy." If your daughter has developed a habit of interrupting others, "You need to let other people speak" should never become "You're rude." It should go without saying that words like *stupid* should never be used as descriptors for your children.

This is a tough one. When you're running late and exasperated with a child's intentional foot-dragging, it's easy to blurt out, "You are so stubborn!" But it's worth every effort to watch your words of criticism carefully. Let your kids know you're on their team. Share responsibility for the problem ("Let's find a good organizational system for you"). And do your best to bookend your criticisms with words of love and affirmation.

If Thou Can't Say Something Nice...

Obviously, it's important to speak words that build your children up and to resist words that break them down. But it's also vital to your kids' sanity that you preserve the unity of your entire family by choosing to speak positively about other family members. When you say hurtful things to or about your spouse, children, parents, or siblings, you sabotage your children's sense of peace and security.

NUMBERS GAME

What percentage of your comments to your children would you say are positive? More than 50%? Less? Much less? Today, keep an index card in your pocket and tally up your criticisms and words of affirmation. Does it look like things are balanced, or do you offer a few more negative comments than positive? Make plans today to shift the ratio more toward the positive.

Researchers report that children whose parents' relationship was characterized by harsh personal criticisms of each other and of third parties not present—like "Why would I listen to what *you* have to say?" and "You're such a liar"—often experience social and emotional problems like anxiety, insecurity, and trouble forming relationships. Says psychologist Clifford Notarius, "You can't just say anything you want. Getting a thicker skin doesn't work in a marriage. It doesn't work in a family, either."[2]

If you berate your spouse or other family members even once, you'll have to work hard to reaffirm them and regain their trust, and even harder to restore a sense of security to your kids. And if you make negative comments regularly, you'll need to make even greater efforts to cleanse the climate in your house. The truth is that you may need help—there's no shame in seeking some level of counseling to help you learn better ways to communicate. On the contrary, seeking help will signify to your kids that you value them and are willing to do whatever is necessary to make their home a safe, comforting place.

Thou Shalt Not Be Untruthful

One of your main goals in improving and maintaining the way you communicate is to model for your kids what good communication looks like. And if you can't insist that your kids tell the truth in situations in which you don't tell the truth yourself.

If you don't want your kids to lie to their teachers, you can't let them catch you lying to your boss. If you don't want them to lie to you, you can't let them catch you lying to your spouse.

Plus, if all relationships are built on trust, you undercut your relationship with your kids when you lie to them, because you give them reason to doubt your word. Don't tell your son you can't play ball with him because you have to mow the lawn if you have every intention of watching TV instead. Don't tell your daughter the reason she can't have a dog is that you're allergic if the real reason is that you just don't want one. Kids are more perceptive than you think, but even if they never figure out that you're skirting the truth, your relationship with them has been compromised, which puts you in a difficult position. In the words of Mark Twain, "If you tell the truth you don't have to remember anything."

Thou Shalt Not Make Unreasonable Demands

You probably ask your children to do fifty things a day—take out the trash, let the dog out, unload the dishwasher. What you never want to do is ask them to do something they can't or imply that what they've accomplished isn't good enough. If your preteen has less-than-stellar athletic ability at this awkward stage in his life and lands a spot on the second-string basketball team, you won't help the situation by asking, "Why didn't you make the starting five?"

Also in this category is the tendency we have, especially

when we're frustrated or angry, to toss out resigned, unrealistic demands, saying things like, "Why can't you be more like your sister?" to your middle daughter or, "I don't understand why you can't make straight A's," to your C student.

Of course you should challenge and encourage your child to reach new heights. And it's true that if you set the bar high and believe they can accomplish something, they're likely to do it. But by setting them up to fall short of your expectations, you set them up to experience the kind of painful discouragement that will keep them from trying new things in the future.

Thou Shalt Forgive Thyself and Move On

You might be feeling a little guilty right now. It's horrifyingly easy to slip up and say something hurtful, maybe especially to our spouse and kids. They so often catch us at our weakest moments. Plus, all of us have picked up the methodologies and phrases of our parents— some good, some not so good—and we so often catch ourselves parroting the things we heard as children. And on top of all that, we're simply human: We do and say the wrong thing sometimes.

If you're upset over past mistakes, rest assured that you'll make new ones—and that your mistakes are not fatal.

Plus, it is possible to change our behavior and give our

family interactions a makeover. "I grew up in a house filled with lots of anger and finger pointing," said Kevin. "I couldn't understand why my wife thought I was mad—and the kids were so unresponsive—when I repeated those patterns. I didn't know what I sounded like.

"The best single piece of advice I ever received was 'attack the problem, not the person.' It has literally changed my relationship with my wife and kids. When I hear my volume going up, it's my cue to slow down and deal with the problem firmly but quietly."

It takes work and self-control to watch our words and tone. In the words of

WHEN YOU'VE BLOWN IT...

Here are a few tips for getting back on track if you've said things you regret.

• Ask your child to forgive you. Don't feel as if you need to recite an entire litany of every hurtful thing you've ever said, but do let your kids know that you recognize that your words have hurt them and that you want to do better for them in the future.

• Forgive yourself. Don't get bogged down in past mistakes. Move on.

• Take steps to improve. It's possible you'll need help from a counselor to stop lashing out at your family. Or it's possible you've already gotten all the reality check you need to recognize how your words are affecting your kids. In any case, commit to watching what you say.

the Bible, "The mouth speaks the things that are in the heart" (Matthew 12:34). Keeping our words helpful and loving means maintaining a soft heart toward our kids and putting their needs above our own—no easy task sometimes. But as they get older, we'll see the fruits of our efforts to speak positively and helpfully to our kids.

PERSONAL REFLECTION:

What do you think is your biggest weakness when it comes to speaking to your children? Do you ever compare? Do you criticize more than you affirm? Is it hard for you to verbally express affection?

YOUR TO DO LIST:

Make a list of five great things about each of your kids. Look for opportunities to tell your children what you like about them in the coming days.

FOR FURTHER STUDY:

Hidden Messages: What Our Words and Actions Are Really Telling Our Children
—by Elizabeth Pantley

The Power of a Parent's Words
—by H. Norman Wright

Hearing Is Believing: How Words Can Make or Break Our Kids
—by Elisa Medhus, M.D.

CHAPTER 4

Spiritual Nurture

*As I contemplate the kind of future I want
for children—my own and other people's—
I believe we must look inward to God
for guidance and strength and backwards
to draw on the values and legacies of our
families, ancestors, and communities.*

—MARIAN WRIGHT EDELMAN

POWER STATEMENT:

Raising kids is incomplete
without nurturing their spirits
as well as their bodies and
minds.

A day in the life of the typical family is pretty hectic—lunches to pack, rides to coordinate, soccer practice, work, housework. So much energy is directed toward the mundane responsibilities of life that it's easy to forget that we have another goal as parents: to nurture our kids' souls as well as their bodies and minds.

The truth is that spirituality is not really the icing on the parenthood cake—it's closely bound up with the overall health of our children. We do something for our kids' spirits by keeping them physically safe and healthy and emotionally secure; but our kids' spirits really take flight when we make the spiritual life of our families a priority and teach our kids to take care of their souls.

A lot of us approach the spiritual element of our family lives with questions and uncertainty. First of all, where do we begin? And what if our kids see our attempts to instill a respect for the spiritual as oppressive and restrictive and give up on religion and spirituality altogether?

Nonetheless, we can't afford not to give our kids spiritual direction. It's such a vital aspect of their lives, and they need us to help them find their course. We can't merely transfer our beliefs to our children; but we can instill in them a rich inner life, point them in the right direction, and in the process give their lives a sense of purpose and meaning.

Phase One: Determine Your Priorities

Where to begin? You have a few things in mind—you'd like your kids to make good decisions and treat people with respect, as well as enjoy the things about spirituality that make your own life vibrant and meaningful. But how do you get there?

It's time to ask yourself, "What kind of spiritual lives do I want my children to have?" What beliefs do you want to pass on to your kids? Are you mostly concerned with their character and value system? Or are you mostly concerned that they have rich spiritual experiences?

Your kids need guideposts in several areas—

Morality and Character Formation

Character isn't just about *not* stealing or *not* cheating; it's more about striving for excellence in every aspect of our being. A kid with strong character doesn't cheat, not because he'll disappoint his parents and teachers if he gets caught, but because to do so would be to lie to himself and cheat himself out of an opportunity for excellence. It's tricky to teach morals as something deeper than pleasing or displeasing authority figures, but it can and should be done.

What *values* do you most want to instill in your children? Honesty? Perseverance and hard work?

Empathy? It might help you to do some careful thinking and make a written list of the character traits you think are most important.

Spiritual Experience

You've probably had some unique spiritual experiences in your life—experiences which may have dictated much of the direction your life has taken. Maybe you're concerned that your kids enjoy the experience of belonging to a faith community as you have. Maybe you want your kids to experience worship in some of the ways that have been most meaningful to you. Or maybe you'd like them to seek counsel through prayer and feel that prayer makes a difference in their lives.

Write out the spiritual experiences you'd most like your kids to have. You won't be able to force your kids to experience the things you have in the exact same way you have, but you can certainly facilitate those experiences and tell your kids what they have meant to you.

Quality of Life

There are certain questions every human being wrestles with, and very often, faith lends our lives a sense of security and meaning. It doesn't always answer every question, but it does help sustain us when life gets tough. Plus, faith can give our lives purpose and direction. What aspects of faith and spirituality do you most want to pass on to your kids in order to help them live full, rich lives? A sense that God is watching out for their future? A sense that they'll receive strength to handle whatever life throws at them?

Once you've got some ideas outlined on all three of these areas, you'll probably notice that nearly everything on your list has to do with the beliefs your kids hold—who they believe God is, what they believe are the important things in life.

Time to make another list. What beliefs do you want to pass on to your children? What beliefs about God and people do you want to mold your kids' ideas about character and spirituality?

Just to state the obvious, you cannot make your children believe everything you believe. For one thing, spirituality is only of value if it incorporates every aspect of our being, not just the part of us that wants to please our parents. Plus, if your kids hold certain beliefs solely with reference to you, they'll be without a compass once it's time to be independent of you. But it is your responsibility to teach your kids beliefs that will equip them to make good decisions and lead lives of significance and purpose. The good news is that it's well within your power to do so.

Phase Two: Intentionally Create a Lifestyle

Meeting your goals for your kids' spiritual lives won't just happen—you'll have to intentionally build an atmosphere in your home that fosters your goals.

An important first step in imparting spiritual principles is to model them for your kids. Again, not an easy task. To model morals and values, do we have to be perfect? If we set up and endorse certain spiritual experiences, will that make us appear holier-than-thou and hypocritical? Most of us are a little uncomfortable with taking on a spiritual guru persona; is it possible to model spiritual principles without having all the answers?

Relax. Modeling is about nurturing your kids' spiritual lives by nurturing your own. And as it turns out, taking care of your soul is probably what will most make your parenting strong and effective.

Look at the list of the moral principles you want to instill in your kids and try to assess how you're doing in each area. Are you modeling honesty for your kids—returning extra change to the cashier when they undercharge you, always being truthful to your kids, spouse, and others? Do you model perseverance, taking your son golfing and letting him see you finish eighteen holes, even after you shot eighty on the first nine?

What about spiritual activities? If you want to raise kids who value church, do you attend regularly and enthusiastically? If you want them to value prayer, do you weave prayer into your family life and pray on your own?

A few additional principles on modeling include—

- Be intentional. Look for and create opportunities to model the things you most want to pass on to your kids.

- Explain your actions. If you try to model compassion by mowing the lawn for an elderly neighbor, explain that you're doing so because you want to help her with the things she can't do for herself.

- Don't be too hard on yourself. If you feel like you're failing to model the things you'd like to teach your kids, don't beat yourself up—or try to cover up your flaws and present a front of spiritual perfection to your kids. Your kids need to know that spirituality is not a contest with winners and losers.

Of course, in addition to modeling spiritual principles for your kids, there's a time to teach them directly as well. If you look for them, you'll find all kinds of opportunities to teach your kids the importance of hard work or compassion, and it's great to create your own learning experiences as well.

You may be bursting with ideas about how to teach your kids values; or you may be struggling with how to present lofty concepts like patience to young kids. Here are a few tips on teaching five important character traits:

Compassion

- When you watch TV with your kids, look for opportunities to discuss how the characters may be thinking and feeling. This will help them get into the practice of acknowledging what others might be feeling and acting considerately.

- Pick a Saturday to go through closets and toy boxes to pull out clothes that are too small or toys that are no longer played with and take the items to a charitable organization, making sure to tell your kids where their old toys and clothes will be going. (An extra bonus to this activity: Your closets will be a lot cleaner!)

- Invest in some sparkly gold stickers. Every time you see one of your kids doing something nice for someone else, let him or her wear a sticker for the day.

Honesty

- Don't force your kids to do or say something they don't mean—don't tell them to kiss their aunt if they really don't want to.

- If you catch a kid stretching the truth, discuss the long-term consequences of lying to someone, i.e., when you lie, you have to remember every detail of the lie indefinitely. Remember that particularly when they're younger, kids tend to lose touch with the hard-and-fast facts when they're telling a story, so make a distinction between "embellishing" and deliberately lying for personal gain. If they're just exaggerating without even realizing it, gently talk them through the facts, explaining how important it is to get the story straight.

- When playing games together, talk about the importance of playing honestly. Highlight a few discussion questions: What happens to the game if someone cheats? If you cheat and win, have you really won?

Patience

- Implement an allowance plan and help your kids find a toy or activity to save up for. This will help them understand that some things don't come immediately and require us to persevere.

- Let kids help with a project that will take time. You can choose anything from baking bread to refinishing furniture, just as long as it takes time and you allow your kids to enjoy the end result.

Commitment

- If a toy breaks, try to fix it or use the parts for something else.

- When your kids want to join a club or sign up for an activity, make sure they stick with it for as long as it's reasonable to do so. If they want to quit, have them stick it out for a semester.

- Be consistent and committed with your family rituals, whether it's Sunday lunches or family game night on Thursdays.

Fairness

- Use charts to determine whose turn it is to help with various chores around the house.

- Look for opportunities to demonstrate fairness. In the inevitable skirmishes that occur between kids over a toy or game, ask them what they think is a fair way to make sure they each get a turn.

Fill your home with opportunities for spiritual growth, either through subtle examples or structured activities, and you're that much closer to meeting your goals for developing your kids' character and encouraging them to look toward the spiritual. But the glue that holds it all together happens when you help your kids develop their belief system.

Teaching Beliefs: Toolbox

Take a look at your list of the beliefs you want to pass on to your kids. You're probably neither a theology professor nor a monk, so where do you begin? Two things to keep in mind: First of all, you're not alone—there are churches and classes and possibly even family members ready to help you. Also, you have plenty of teaching tools at your disposal that will make your job a whole lot easier.

Church

Your place of worship will be your greatest ally in helping your children develop spiritual beliefs. A lot of churches have great kids' programs that help kids learn religious principles as well as elements of good character in a way that accommodates young attention spans. Plus, very often it's a place of worship that offers you and your kids a community that nurtures spiritual development.

Here are a few keys to making church a growing experience for your kids—and you:

- Find a good fit for your family. Choose a place where you and your kids feel comfortable enough to get involved, and it would probably be a good idea to audit your kids' church classes a few times and open the lines of communication with their teachers to get an idea of what your kids are learning.

- Reinforce what your kids learn in church at home. Ask them to tell you what they learned after each class—putting it in their own words will help them grasp the concepts. Make it easy for your kids to do any "homework" they may have by encouraging them and setting aside time in their schedule.

- You'll help your kids' teachers and volunteers do their jobs by getting involved. Involvement doesn't mean selling your soul to the youth group; it just means being available to bring snacks a few times or host a holiday party. Ask workers what they most need from you as a parent. Plus, getting involved is a key to your own spiritual development at church as well.

Family Time

As important and helpful as church is, you are the greatest spiritual influence in your child's life. As such, the efforts you make to teach them beliefs and values are incredibly important, and the time you set aside to discuss spiritual matters goes farther than you might realize.

Instituting a family devotion time might seem a little scary (you're probably already anticipating the eye rolls from your teens), but it can be done gracefully. Here are a few ideas.

- Make use of both formal and informal opportunities for spiritual discussions. Life is full of object lessons, especially with older kids.

- If you're ready to start a regular, organized family prayer time, start slow, easing your family into the new routine. You might start with just prayer once a week, then begin adding new elements of study and discussion.

- Time things right. Pick a time of day that will work for your whole family, like dinnertime or bedtime. Be mindful of your little ones' attention spans when determining how long to make your family time.

- Choose the elements you think will best meet your goals. Read from a family devotion book, or simply read a scripture or verse and pray together. Keep things discussion-centered—don't force answers or jump in too soon. Rather, let your kids process and discuss the issues at hand.

Books, Videos, etc.

While the responsibility to teach your kids can never be passed off to Mr. Rogers and Sesame Street, you'll find that you have a lot of help available in the form of videos, books, and tapes that teach spiritual principles in a fun way.

One fun pick is Max Lucado's *Hermie & Friends*™ series from Tommy Nelson®. These books and videos teach lessons on truth, friendship, following the rules, and more with colorful images and easy-to-follow storylines. With a variety of products and formats, this series presents truths about God and life while also including fun games, songs, and clever subtleties even grownups will appreciate.

Holidays

Holidays present a unique opportunity to teach your kids about their spiritual heritage: Their attention is piqued due to their anticipation of celebrations (which usually involve candy), and most holidays signify the importance of a particular religious principle or historic event with spiritual significance. There are a few things you'll want to consider:

- Make your traditions useful, and explain the significance of each. There's nothing wrong with goofy traditions—they build the fun factor in your holiday celebrations and boost your family's feeling of solidarity—but make sure you have a few traditions in place that reinforce the historical meaning of the holiday. Be creative and feel free to invent new traditions if need be.

- Put on your teacher hat and tell your kids the history behind the holidays. Tell the Nativity story at Christmas, or the Hanukkah story at Hanukkah, highlighting the spiritual importance of holiday stories.

- Make use of symbols. Kids respond very well to teaching tools that incorporate multiple senses. So heavily feature visual reminders of the spiritual significance of holidays in your celebrations: nativity scenes, crosses, lights and candles.

Spiritual training is a vital aspect of raising kids. But it's important to recognize that if the other components of your parenting are falling apart, your spiritual goals will be largely unmet. Translation: If you lead your family in prayer time and make a point of modeling integrity, but fail to nurture a loving relationship with your spouse and kids, you'll have a much harder time getting the spiritual

CASE STUDY:

Robert, age forty-six, faced a major dilemma. He grew up a preacher's kid and his dad was a very prominent leader in the denomination he and his family had loyally attended for generations. The problem?

"My sixteen-year-old son had all but lost interest in spiritual matters," he said. "But that changed when he went on a weekend retreat with four of his best friends that attended another church. He came home fired up for God like we hadn't seen in years. So we let him go to the Wednesday night Bible studies at a different church because he loved it so much.

"Now he wants to attend church there on Sundays. I want him to be where he grows. But I want my family together at church. Honestly, I don't know what to do, but I'm inclined to let him attend there. I know my dad won't be happy, but that's another issue."

There will always be decisions to make regarding our kids' spiritual development, and some of those decisions won't be easy. But as we seek to do what's best for our kids' spiritual lives, if nothing else, we model for them what it means to make spirituality a priority, and we get them that much closer to having a rich spiritual life.

principles to stick.

But be encouraged as you take steps today to care for your own soul as well as your children's, knowing that your efforts are paying off toward building a strong spiritual foundation for your kids that will serve them the rest of their lives.

PERSONAL REFLECTION:

What kind of spiritual upbringing did you have as a child? What do you want to emulate about your childhood? What do you want to do differently? Why do you think you have the priorities that you do?

YOUR TO DO LIST:

What's one discipline you can implement in your own life this week? More consistent church attendance? Is there a personal spiritual discipline you've been meaning to adopt? Put it into practice and set a goal to be consistent for at least six weeks.

FOR FURTHER STUDY:

The Values Book
— by Pam Schiller and Tamera Bryant

C H A P T E R 5

Establishing Boundaries

A child who is allowed to be disrespectful to his parents will not have true respect for anyone.

—BILLY GRAHAM

POWER STATEMENT:

Establishing boundaries is about teaching kids to respect themselves and others.

What's true in life in general is true in parenting: If you don't set boundaries for yourself, others will set them for you. We do ourselves and our kids a huge favor when we provide a structure for our kids to live in, teaching them to use self-discipline and respect themselves and others.

Kids need boundaries. We've already discussed a child's need for security, and one of the best ways to give them a sense of security is to set and enforce reasonable limits. Besides, in order for kids to grow up and form good relationships, they need to learn early how to respect the rights, needs, and desires of others. And if nothing else, boundaries make family life a whole lot smoother.

Establishing boundaries for you and your kids comes in two parts: helping establish personal boundaries for everyone in your family, and setting limits on your kids' habits and behavior.

Mutual Respect

Implementing family boundaries starts by evaluating and establishing our own personal set of limits. Do parents need boundaries? Absolutely.

For one thing, an important way for parents to teach kids to respect and discipline themselves is to model self-respect and self-discipline. For another thing, while selflessness is an essential of parenting, as parents, we're still human beings, and as such need personal boundaries. It's tempting sometimes to pour so much of our time and energy—so much of ourselves—into our kids that the lines between our own lives and theirs start to blur. And that's not really healthy for anyone.

It's not selfish or unloving to maintain our personal separateness. We need to keep control of our time, being careful to allow ourselves some downtime and not to overcommit ourselves. It won't scar your kids for life for you to gently tell them, "Mom's going to read for a little while. Why don't you go play with your sister?"

According to Drs. Henry Cloud and John Townsend, maintaining personal boundaries is about ownership: Taking responsibility for our beliefs, activities, thoughts, and values. Not only is it important to our emotional stability to understand our limits and take initiative with our lives, it also models for our kids how to do the same.

There's an area of our family lives that especially needs to be guarded and that we're often tempted to neglect: our marriage. As easy as it is to become engrossed in your kids' activities, your marriage should fuel your parenting, not revolve around your parenting—even with kids in the picture, your marriage should maintain its separate integrity.

During those crazy-busy years in the thick of parenting, marriage gurus David and Claudia Arp recommend keeping a little time exclusive to maintaining your marriage: Spend the first five minutes of the day connecting over coffee, or plan a romantic twenty-four-hour getaway.[1] It might take a little creativity, but it's important to nurture your marriage independently of your kids.

Just as you draw your personal boundaries and seek to nourish your marriage, it's important to give your kids a sense that they're important and worthy of respect as well. And as it turns out, nurturing your kids' personal boundaries and establishing your own go hand in hand.

The key to teaching your kids principles of boundaries is to respect their space, ideas, and wants—doing so will not only show your kids that you think they're important, but also model for them how to respect others. Knock on your child's door before entering. Respect their time by not making last-minute demands on them. Respect their belongings.

A common battleground between parents and their kids when it comes to respecting others is interrupting. Most parents make an effort to teach their kids not to interrupt when an adult is talking. And that's a great idea—even though it's a tough principle to put into practice (adults can talk for an awfully long time, in case you hadn't noticed), it's great to teach kids to respect other's conversations and to be polite in their dealings with other people. But you'll really hit the respect lesson home when you allow your child to talk without interrupting.

By respecting your kids and respecting yourself, you teach them to consider other people's needs and point of view as well as be mindful of their own. And that kind of mutual respect will serve your kids both at home and at school, as well as in the future.

Know the Limit

No one can go through life getting everything they want the second they want it; we all have to learn to delay gratification. And kids won't learn to limit themselves in life unless

WHEN AND HOW TO SAY NO

We've all been there—the grocery store meltdown, the tantrum in front of friends. Here are a few ideas from Jody Johnston Pawel, author of *The Parent's Toolshop: The Universal Blueprint for Building a Healthy Family,* on defusing the situation with a gentle, yet firm no.

- Be sure to give a reason for your no.

- Acknowledge your child's reasoning and feelings, but hold your position.

- Offer a plea bargain: Give a conditional "yes" or suggest an alternative.

- Let the child choose one from several options.

they learn to live within limits at home.

There are several things to consider as you set out to set limits for your kids. First of all, it's important to try to see the bigger picture. The purpose of your limits is not to keep your kids from neglecting their homework or eating candy instead of dinner; the purpose of limits is to teach your kids to take responsibility for themselves, to consider the consequences of their actions, and to make decisions based on respect for others.

And so, your goal as a parent is not just to create and enforce rules. You'll serve your kids much better by being a little more hands-on—giving them an allowance and helping them live within a budget, or helping them hammer out a soccer training schedule and working out with them.

Something else to remember is that as much as kids need limits, they need love more. And you'll have far more success in motivating them if your relationship is grounded in love and security.

When it comes time to lay down the law, there are a few rules to go by—

- Be realistic. Take your kids' ages into consideration (see Chapter 9), and be careful not to set the limits out of your kids' reach. Establishing a rule about cookies before dinner is fine; expecting kids to make it to dinner without a snack after school is probably not.

- Be clear. It's critical that the limits you set be communicated clearly and in advance. A set of house rules is great, and for those more specific limits like TV watching, just be sure your kids know what your expectations are.

- Be consistent. It's also critical that you enforce the limits you set. Prohibiting certain kinds of movies and TV shows does no good unless you take steps to enforce the rule.

- Be bold. As important as it is to respect your kids' needs and wants, there are times when you have to be the bad guy. If your daughter wants to have a friend sleep over on a Tuesday, but you've set a limit on having friends over after 8:30 p.m. on school nights, it's best to stick to your guns. The trick is to listen to your daughter's reasoning and express empathy, but explain that the rule is in place for a reason.

Apply healthy limits for your kids, and you'll find yourself doing something more important than just setting limits: You'll be building their character.

PERSONAL REFLECTION:

How do you think you're doing in terms of establishing and maintaining boundaries? Are your personal boundaries clear? Do you make efforts to respect your kids' space and personality? What do you think is your weakest point in terms of setting limits?

✓ YOUR TO DO LIST:

One of the great things about hobbies is that they provide an opportunity for kids to take personal responsibility for a task. Maybe today would be a good day to take your child out to look for an age-appropriate hobby—collecting coins, painting, a favorite sport, anything that sparks your child's interest.

FOR FURTHER STUDY:

Boundaries with Kids
—by Drs. Henry Cloud and John Townsend

Setting Limits with Your Strong-Willed Child: Eliminating Conflict by Establishing Clear, Firm, and Respectful Boundaries
—by Robert J. MacKenzie, Ed.D.

Building Healthy Self-Esteem

---

*Nothing builds self-esteem
and self-confidence like accomplishment.*

—THOMAS CARLYLE

POWER STATEMENT:

We can't simply give our
kids self-esteem, but
we can give them a sense of
love and acceptance and
help them earn self-esteem.

It's possible that there is no hotter topic on the parenting bookshelf than self-esteem. Some would say self-esteem is the single most important goal of parenting; others would say it's overrated at best. So what does a healthy self-image look like?

Low self-esteem has long been associated with all kinds of psychological and emotional problems. But it doesn't take much research to discover that kids who see themselves as worthwhile, valuable people are likely to set and achieve goals and handle problems with a minimum of emotional distress, while kids who have an underdeveloped sense of their significance and value will likely hesitate to take risks and become easily defeated. Elementary school students categorized as having low self-esteem, for example, often hesitate to express unpopular ideas in class, tend to be low achievers, and often lag behind in terms of achieving independence.

Obviously, it's important for kids to have a basic sense that they are valuable and appreciated, something they can best get from their parents. As kids leave infancy and begin to conceive of themselves as separate, individual entities, they also begin to adopt a sense of value of themselves, which they absorb largely from the significant people in their lives. Put another way, every child will form some sort of self-image; whether that self-image is one that enables him or her to meet challenges and thrive depends on us as parents.

And the job isn't done when kids leave for school. As they get older and are exposed to media images and other pressures, kids can become tempted to judge their worth in terms of how well they conform to popular ideals. But parents who make their kids feel loved and important can lend them a sense of value despite the things that seek to hurt a child's self-image.

Where to Begin

So what's the best way to approach the nurturing of a child's self-esteem? A good place to start is to examine our own hearts and lives. For one thing, studies show that adults with healthy self-esteem usually raise children with healthy self-esteem. A sense of self-worth is usually more easily modeled than taught, and plus, it's easy to unfairly transfer our insecurities about ourselves onto our kids.

For another thing, in order to communicate to our kids that they're valuable, we need to recognize and deeply believe that they are. Do we appreciate our kids' uniquenesses, or do we inwardly criticize them for not being as athletic or funny or outgoing as we wanted them to be? Do we truly value our kids above our possessions and ambitions, or do we sometimes get preoccupied and lose sight of whether their needs are being met? Chances are that you adore your kids—but every now and then we need to remind ourselves how precious they really are.

All good parents want what's best for their kids, and that includes a healthy self-image. But how, in the middle of our day-to-day routines, do we build their self-esteem?

The truth is that no one can *give* their child self-esteem. In many ways, self-esteem is something that must be earned as children conquer new tasks and experience a variety of successes. But we as parents can give our kids a sense of acceptance and intrinsic worth, as well as provide opportunities for them to develop confidence in their abilities.

There are lots of words and actions that will communicate to your child, "You are important to me." To make your child feel wanted, simply tell her she is: "I'm so glad you're in our family." Let your kids know how they make your life better and how they bring you joy. Another way to convey to your kids a feeling that they're important is to give them your time, taking an interest in their school activities and taking the time to listen to their concerns, stories, and thoughts.

Feeling that they matter to you is vital to your kids—it's what will keep them from having a total breakdown when they fail at something. And you'll help your kids sail even more smoothly by setting them up to experience success.

Five Things
You Can Do *Today*
to Nurture
Your Child's Self-Image

- Tell your child, "I'm so glad you're my son," or "I'm so glad you're my daughter."

- Take him out on a "date"—go see a movie or go to the park for a picnic, just the two of you.

- Go to a game or activity in which she is participating.

- Stick a note to their mirror which reads, "Five Things I Love About You."

- Provide an opportunity for your child to do something himself—build a hamster maze, do an art project, pick out an outfit.

Affirm your kids when you notice them doing something well—and actively try to "catch" them doing things well. Let them know they're unique and have things to offer the world.

But what may be even more important than what you say is what your child experiences. If he wins the toothpick bridge-building contest, he'll know he's good at solving problems. If her teachers love her paintings, she'll know she's artistic. So it's important to help your kids find their strengths. Give them lots of opportunities to try new things, and encourage them when they find their sweet spot. Celebrate successes, and let them know it's okay when they fail.

Something else to think about as we try to help our kids meet challenges is how high to set our expectations. We convey to our kids that they're competent and capable by setting our expectations fairly high, expecting them to meet appropriate levels of independence and achievement. But it's also important that we not set our expectations too high, thereby communicating to our kids that they aren't what we hoped they were.

So maybe it's not possible to simply transfer self-esteem to our kids; but it certainly is possible to provide an environment where a child's self-image can thrive.

What *Not* to Do

Obviously, just as a parent has great power to build a child's self-esteem, he or she can have a negative impact on a child's self-image as well.

Of course, none of us want to make our kids feel bad about themselves, and it's unlikely that we'll do irrevocable damage by accident. Still, there are some pitfalls we need to watch out for. It's important, for example, that we make every effort to make a distinction between a child and his actions. When addressing a bad report card, it's important for a parent to keep a cool head and try to determine what might be the root of the problem, rather than berating a child and demanding that she "do better." When punishing one of your kids, qualifying, "you are bad" statements need to be avoided, since they can make kids see themselves as bad and generally displeasing.

It's also important to be careful about teasing our kids. It's one thing to rib our kids a little in a good-natured, familiar way, but in a child's mind, a little teasing can lean a little too closely toward ridicule and humiliation. Be careful about teasing your kid in front of his peers, and for every time you tease your kids about their lateness or talkativeness, make sure you let them know something you genuinely like about them. And, always, think before you speak, asking yourself, "Is this worth it?" How big a risk is there that this or that comment will hurt your child's self-esteem, and is it worth an easy joke?

What may be even worse than low self-esteem, though, is hollow self-esteem. With self-esteem rising to the forefront of parenting and educational concerns in recent years, says Michael K. Meyerhoff, some parents and teachers are adopting an "everybody wins" mentality in an effort to keep kids from failure. Unfortunately, this doesn't accomplish real self-esteem at all, since it doesn't provide an opportunity for a child to prove to himself that he's really good at something.[1]

So, rather than take our kids out of competitive

situations altogether, we should seek to help them achieve. If your child fails at soccer, help him find an activity in which he really excels. (And by no means yank him out of soccer if he enjoys playing and being part of the team.) It's not necessarily important that he be the absolute best at something, but it is important that he feels that he's truly good at it.

Self-esteem can be tricky. It's something kids need, and yet bad versions of self-esteem can cause problems, to say the least—kids can become accustomed to too much praise and not be able to function in the real world, or they may not have the confidence they need to make strides in life. Plus, our own view of ourselves can complicate our efforts to guide our kids to a healthy self-image. But really, when it comes to building self-esteem, all that's required of us is to love and respect our kids and help them learn to engage the world. It's not an easy job—but our kids will thank us later.

PERSONAL REFLECTION:

Has self-esteem been an issue in your own life? What in your life has helped or hurt your view of yourself? How do you think your kids are doing?

CASE STUDY:

One myth of building self-esteem is that actions and accomplishments don't matter—some parents feel that verbal affirmation is all a kid needs to feel good about herself. The problem is that when we say "good job" even when a child hasn't done a good job, he'll know we aren't being totally truthful. Consequently, when we affirm him for real accomplishments, he won't really believe you.

Sarah, a mother of a fourteen-year-old boy, said, "I wanted to be both affirming and honest to boost Kevin's self-esteem, but I wasn't always sure how to go about it. What turned things around was noticing how much he enjoyed collecting and organizing things—not his room, of course, but little knickknacks and things. So one day, I went to the hobby store with him and bought him a stamp book, plus a beginner's guide to collecting stamps. He took to it like a duck to water and over the past three years has built five books and has actually developed a valuable collection because he studies it so extensively. Best of all, encouraging him to do something he was good at did wonders for his self-esteem—he's a really happy kid."

✓ *YOUR TO DO LIST:*

Sometimes the world beats your kids down, and that's when they need you to let them know they're okay. Make a few preemptive strikes today by letting them know you love, care for, and enjoy them.

FOR FURTHER STUDY:

Hide or Seek
—by Dr. James Dobson

CHAPTER  **7**

Letting Go

The greatest gifts you can give your children
are the roots of responsibility
and the wings of independence.

—DENIS WAITLEY

POWER STATEMENT:

Letting go begins the day
we bring them home, and
never quite stops.

It can be tough to let go. It's not easy to know when to step in and when to let your child fend for himself. Besides that, it sometimes simply hurts. It hurts to see our kids enduring painful circumstances, and it hurts when they move away from us, physically or emotionally.

We can't eliminate all risk and pain from our children's lives, and they can't stay children forever. But letting go is easier when we take steps to prepare our kids to face the world and prepare ourselves to deal with change.

Helping Them Chart Their Course

One of the most important aspects of letting go is giving our kids the tools they need to face the world, and teaching them to take initiative and responsibility for their own lives. Sometimes, much to our dismay, that involves taking a "hands off" approach, letting them find their own way.

In certain cultures, so they say, as a rite of passage into manhood, a boy is sent into the jungle with nothing but a spear to kill the lion and return victorious. On the opposite end of the letting-go spectrum, some parents do everything for their kids until the day they leave for college (or later) and wonder why their young adult flounders in the real world—or seems disinclined to leave home at all. The best approach has to be somewhere between these two extremes, but how do we find it?

One key to growing capable, competent kids is to pace ourselves. Our kids' experience with responsibility shouldn't be a steep grade, but more like a gradual climb—one that starts early. The goal is to give them plenty of age-appropriate choices, responsibilities, and

Tools for Teaching Responsibility

- Allowance. Determine an appropriate, affordable amount to give your child each week. Help them pick out something they'd like to save up for. And be clear from the beginning—there will be no advances and no bonuses.

- Pets. This is a tricky one. On one hand, pets are great because they give kids a shot at responsibility as well as lots of fun and unconditional love. On the other hand, you roll the dice when you get a pet for your kid—things may not work out, and then you're left with lots of expenses and a problem pet, which is unfair to the animal and hard for the child. So do your research, and give careful consideration to what kind of pet your child might be ready for.

- Chores. Ah, chores. Chores are a perfect parenting tool: They're free, effective, and if that's not enough, they get you that much closer to getting the housework done. Choose a few tasks for your kids to do, things they're physically capable of doing. You might consider a chore chart where kids can check off what they've done and work toward a reward of some kind.

freedoms. Let your toddler choose between the red shirt and the green shirt. Make sure your six-year-old is responsible for dressing himself in the morning. Allow your preteen to go places by herself (within the limits of safety, of course).

Letting go, letting our kids take the reins in various areas of their lives, is particularly important as they enter their teen years. Nowhere is this principle more clearly illustrated than in the phenomenon of "Daddy's girl" syndrome: Young women hit their twenties without budgeting skills, having spent their lives with Dad as their financial safety net—paying off their credit cards, paying their cell phone bill, and buying them cars.[1] We just don't do our kids any favors by doing everything for them. You'll do well to live by this credo throughout your kids' lives: Never do for a child what he can do for himself.

Plus, kids need hands-on opportunities to learn to take responsibility, which they can only get when we allow them to do things for themselves. Teach them to manage money by allowing them to manage some money. Teach them to take care of their belongings by giving them responsibility over their belongings.

Audrey, with twin boys who were struggling in school, finally had to admit she was part of the problem. She had constantly "nagged"—her word—the boys to make their beds, pick up their room, clear the table after dinner, and a host of other chores. But she found it much easier to do the work herself than make sure they did it themselves.

"Fifth grade was an eye opener for the boys and me," she said. "Now they had real work every single night and they didn't know how to stay on task. I was tempted to just do things for them, but I realized that if they were going to succeed, they needed to develop a work ethic. So I refused to do the work for them, and tried to give their homework time some structure.

"It was tough and we still struggle. But watching them finish a task is so worth the effort."

It's not always easy to get kids to take responsibility. Sometimes they consistently forget their lunch or their jacket—what does a parent do then? Let them freeze on the playground? We don't want our kids to suffer for being forgetful or late, but there are times when we need to allow them to experience the consequences of their actions.

Nancy Samalin suggests explaining to kids what you expect of them and holding them to your expectations. If you tell your child that he's responsible for remembering to grab his lunch off the counter and he calls at 11:00 to tell you he forgot, don't bring him his lunch. Let him down easy: "Be gracious about it, don't blame, but be firm."[1] Alison Rees, a counselor and educator in Victoria, British Columbia, agrees. We can't shield our child from consequences, but rather, "our job is to make sure the consequences aren't devastating."[2] That's the way kids learn, she says. A little discomfort now is better than a lot of pain later.

Dr. Kevin Leman encourages parents not to forget that pain is a valuable teaching tool and that by removing our children from their struggles, we may "stunt their maturity."[3] Plus, rather than making them feel secure, overprotecting our kids actually makes them more fearful, since they don't have a chance to test and trust their own abilities.

Of course, there's another side to the coin. It's a tough world, and we simply can't send our fledgling adult into the jungle with only a spear. We need to equip our kids with knowledge and prepare them for each new responsibility we give them. Before allowing your preteen to walk to the library by herself, go through a few "what-if" scenarios and have her tell you where she'll be going and when she'll be coming back. This will force her to be deliberate about her plans (and will ease your mind a lot). Likewise, before asking your eight-year-old to take on feeding the goldfish, make sure he knows exactly how to meet your expectations—when and how much to feed the fish.

It's something of a paradox: We need to be an instantly available, loving presence in our kids' lives, but at the same time, our kids need to forge their own way. We can strike the right balance by being involved and aware of what's going on in their lives, while keeping in mind our goal to prepare them for adulthood.

CASE STUDY:

Sandra, age ten, read and loved *The One Hundredth Thing About Caroline* by Lois Lowry. In the story, the preteen title character was responsible for doing her own laundry, and Sandra thought that sounded pretty cool. So she had her mom show her how to work the washer and dryer, measure the soap, and sort clothes by color, and from that point forward, Sandra washed all her own clothes each week.

The truth is that kids like to be challenged and enjoy taking on new things. Don't be afraid to give them new responsibilities.

How to Cope

No matter how hard you work at preparing your kids for each new challenge of life, some days are simply hard— like the first day of school, and pretty much every day after that. The joy we feel at watching our kids grow and test their wings is countered by the pain we feel at not being needed quite so much anymore and seeing our kids stumble. There are times we have to watch our child endure pain, which is the hardest thing we ever have to do.

All we can do is keep things in perspective. It helps to think of our kids as growing, changing people, and to remember that it's healthy for them to separate from us a few degrees at a time. When our teens pull away from us, sometimes with anger and tears, we have to force ourselves to remember that their rejection is developmental and not take it personally (which is much easier said than done).

There are other things we can do to ease the transition. For one thing, we can make efforts to de-stress—work out, do stretches, soak in a hot bath. Part of letting go is releasing ourselves from the pressures and anxiety we feel. Another soul-soother is to cultivate one of our own interests. It's hard to find time for yourself, but you'll do yourself a world of good by taking an hour a week to play racquetball or enroll in a dance class, if for no other reason to remind yourself that there is life outside your kids. The key to successful letting go is to care for ourselves just as we care for our children.

Even as you let go, remember that your kids still need you. Don't stop giving your teen hugs—they need your acceptance and affection now more than ever. Throughout their lives, your kids will need the benefit of your wisdom and experiences as they make their way in the world. And even when they're your age, you'll still hold a very important place in their lives.

PERSONAL REFLECTION:

Is there an area of your kids' lives in which it's particularly hard for you to let go? Are your kids more or less on target in terms of having age-appropriate responsibilities?

✓ *YOUR TO DO LIST:*

Place a little more responsibility on your kids' shoulders this week. Is your six-year-old ready for some pet fish, or your young teen ready to serve lunch to his younger siblings this Saturday? Pick out a new job, responsibility, or freedom for them this week.

FOR FURTHER STUDY:

Ophelia's Mom
    —by Nina Shandler

CHAPTER 8

Discipline

When my kids become wild and unruly,
I use a nice, safe playpen.
When they're finished, I climb out.

—ERMA BOMBECK

POWER STATEMENT:

Discipline is necessary.
Only by disciplining our
kids do we enable them to
discipline themselves.

If you're a new parent, you may feel more terrified and confused about discipline than any other area of parenting. Every time your four-year-old sasses you, you may have visions of an angry teenager with a pierced lip and wonder if that's what awaits you. Or maybe you're intent on avoiding the harshness or permissiveness you grew up with.

But nonetheless, confrontation is simply unavoidable. There are going to be times when you have to discipline your child, and he's not going to like it.

Studies show that children of "permissive" parents—parents who give few if any directives and put no limits on their children's impulses—tend to be impulsive and aggressive and lack self-reliance. At the other extreme, children of "authoritarian" parents—parents who exercise strict control using punishment and shame—tend to be withdrawn and fearful.[1] Kids need a balance, and forgoing discipline altogether is simply not an option.

So where do we start? What do good discipline habits look like, and how do we develop them?

There are a few things we need to realize from the beginning. For one thing, we need to remember that our ultimate goal is to teach our kids self-discipline. By limiting and disciplining our kids, we're not trying to break their will; we're laying the groundwork for them to learn to redirect their will. Ultimately, we're aiming to shape our child's internal motivation, to instill in them a voice that says, "I won't do this because it would hurt someone, and that's wrong," or "I won't do this because if I delay gratification, it will pay off later."

You're going to have to start early—only when kids have had a loving adult set limits on their behavior will they be able to limit their own behavior as they grow up. A lot of parents tend to go a little too easy during their children's first years, forcing them to toughen up as kids head toward middle school, which leads to lots of long, hard discipline battles. The good news is that if we give our kids limits and consistency from an early age, we're less likely to have to use harsher disciplinary measures as they get older.

Our attitude is key. Discipline is so important, and sometimes we want to do things right so badly that we end up becoming almost obsessed with discipline. But discipline shouldn't overshadow every other aspect of our parenting. As Dr. Perri Klass puts it, "If the sum total of life with your child seems to be about saying no and scolding and handing out penalties, then something's gone wrong."[2] Make sure to take the pressure off every now and then with some fun time.

And most importantly, we need to remember that discipline will never be effective outside of a loving relationship. Your kids need to feel connected to you in order to take correction properly, and that connection must be built in your day-in, day-out interactions and habits.

Knowledge is power. Knowing what our kids need and are ready for will guide us as we seek to give our kids loving discipline.

Ages and Stages

Good discipline evolves as kids get older—there's no need to discipline a toddler the way you discipline a ten-year-old. Tailoring our discipline to our kids' age will ensure its effectiveness and save our sanity.

When children are babies, you really can't spoil them. You can't cuddle them too much or be too responsive to their needs. A baby isn't really capable of misbehaving. When they start crawling and toddling, it's time to set some very practical, tangible limits. Babyproof. Say "no" and take away objects they shouldn't play with. Set up a consistent daily routine. And be prepared to repeat yourself.

Toddlers, of course, are a very special discipline case. There are certain things a toddler is biologically, developmentally inclined to do. At this age, they're all about tantrums, short attention spans, and the word "no." Your mission is to set limits they may not understand just yet (they're not quite capable of understanding why it's not okay to hit their friend) and recognize that much of their behavior is developmentally driven.

The way to get through the tantrums is to calm them down and remove them from the situation, without giving in or exploding. You'll also have more success with giving positive rather than negative instructions: "Walk," instead of "Don't run."[3] And on those days where everything's a battle, it's easier said than done, but try not to lose your cool.

As kids get older and enter the preschool years, they're still bundles of energy and emotion, so at this age, it's best to keep up with the routines and repetition you started when your kids were smaller. Keep your rules simple and few, and when you do have to defuse a preschooler's meltdown, be firm. It's also good to keep in mind that young kids don't really have control of their emotions, and sometimes simply they get overwhelmed, so acknowledge their feelings while continuing to limit their behavior: "I know you're disappointed, but it's not okay to throw things."

Once kids are out of kindergarten and into grade school, things settle down a bit, which makes discipline a little smoother. One of the best tools of discipline for kids this age is simple consequences. As discussed in Chapter 5, there are times to let kids suffer the natural consequences of their actions, even if it's a little bit painful to do so. Of course, backtalk and disrespect should be addressed quickly and firmly. And now that they're a little older, they're more capable of understanding, so you can and should explain your reasoning a little more.

From the preteen years on, you're moving your kids toward independence. If you've maintained consistent limits and worked to build a solid, loving connection with your kids, you're in a good position. So don't be afraid to negotiate here and there, which will make kids feel more confident and independent. What's tricky is when your kids get to be older teens and their decisions have more potential to have drastic consequences—it's tough to strike a balance between letting them learn on their own through experience and keeping them out of trouble. There are certainly times to take a hard line, and to paraphrase our parents, they'll thank you later.

Throughout our kids' lives, we'll do well to pay close attention to them, fostering a deep relationship with them and watching to see how they respond to different types of discipline, and give them consistent limits.

Matters of Temperament

No two kids respond to discipline the same way, and it's important for us as parents to learn to work with our kids' temperaments, for our kids' well being as much as effectiveness in discipline.

For one thing, we need to gauge our kids' sensitivity. "Golden retriever" children, as discussed in Chapter 2, tend to take on extra responsibilities and very often feel guilty for things that are not their fault. Because of this sensitivity, they'll probably feel very guilty at even the slightest reproach. You can help your sensitive child take discipline by watching your tone and reaffirming your love for them even as you correct them. Resist the urge to shield your sensitive child from consequences; rather, comfort and console them in the midst of the painful consequences of their actions.

In the same vein, some kids have a tough time adjusting to new situations—these are the "slow to warm up" kids the textbooks are always talking about. What slow to warm up kids need from you is a little extra patience and a little more warning and preparation when you're about to try something new with them. It's also a good idea to break your instructions down into smaller parts to be followed one at a time.[4]

On the other end of the spectrum, some kids are very active with short attention spans, and they need firmer handling and a little extra dose of patience. It's also good to give lots of warnings to more active kids: "In ten minutes, you're going to have to get out of the pool."

Of course, there's the child everyone fears: the kid who tests every limit and screams at his parents. It's funny how intimidating someone two feet tall can be. Dr. James Dobson writes that the key to dealing with a strong-willed child is to be tough. A strong-willed child wants to test you, and you have to prove yourself willing and able to lay down the law and enforce it.[5] But remember that a strong-willed child needs love and affection as much as a compliant child, if not more. Even if you're having a contest of wills every day, don't let a day go by without affirming your strong-willed child in some way.

What Not to Do

Some rules apply regardless of age or temperament. Just as there are some things we should always do, there are some things we should never do.

For one thing, we should never go back on our word. If we say, "This is your last warning before that toy is taken away," and the child re-offends, we have to take the toy away. Our kids will test us, and we have to be careful to prove that we mean what we say.

We should also never withhold affection as a form of punishment, especially with small children. They simply aren't able to interpret our sudden chilliness. Likewise, humiliation is not an appropriate discipline tool. It's one thing to allow a child to experience the consequences of her behavior in front of other people; it's something else to push her into public shame and humiliation, which is nearly always more damaging than helpful.

Tools and Strategies

Dr. T. Berry Brazelton has this to say about the goals of discipline:

> *First, a child's misbehavior must be stopped. Second, the child may need to regain control of his emotions and calm himself down before he is ready for the next steps. Third, he needs to think about what he has done and understand the consequences, including its effects on others. Fourth comes problem solving, and sometimes negotiation or compromise, as a child works toward making reparations. Finally, apologies and forgiveness.* [6]

It's not always easy to know what to do in the heat of the moment. The key is to remember in discipline is that you're looking to limit your child and help him learn to limit himself. Here are a few tools for your discipline arsenal.

- Modeling

How many times have you heard your four-year-old say something that sounded exactly like you? Our kids are always watching us. They learn how to speak, eat, and treat other people by watching us. For that reason, there's just no substitute for modeling, even when our kids are very small—it's hard to convince a toddler not to yell and scream if we constantly resort to yelling and screaming.

Think about what you want to model for your kids, and put it into practice. When you're polite, they learn to be polite. When you share, they learn to share. When you express your anger to them without losing your calm or hurting their feelings, they learn to control their anger. And don't think you have to be perfect—seeing how you handle your mistakes and slip-ups will teach your kids a lot about taking responsibility for their actions.

- Affirmation

This is a big one. Catching our kids being good and encouraging that behavior is one of the most effective things we can do, and really, if we're focusing our disciplinary efforts on correcting misbehavior without acknowledging correct behavior, we're swimming upstream. For one thing, kids are eager to please, and it's important to recognize their efforts. For another thing, affirmation is a positive, active way to let our kids know what good behavior looks like.

Affirming is easy enough: "I appreciate you sharing." "Thank you so much for helping Mommy clean up." "That's so great that you're helping your sister." Be watching for your kids' good behavior, and point it out when they've improved in one area or another. If there's a particular misbehavior you're trying to correct, affirm the opposite behavior. If your eight-year-old likes to deliberately annoy his preteen sister, affirm him when you catch him being nice to her. With a little time and consistency, the good behavior will likely replace the bad.

You can use affirmation to show trust in your kids' abilities and independence, which is a great way to foster responsibility: "You did a great job handling that situation," and "I'm sure you'll do a great job on your own. I'll be right here if you need help." You can also use encouragement to teach your kids values you'd like to instill: "If you keep working, you'll probably get it."[7] All in all, affirmation is a highly valuable tool for shaping a child's behavior.

- Logical consequences

We've discussed how letting our kids experience some negative consequences of behavior that we'd like to correct can teach them more than anything we could ever say. But another good teaching tool is to enforce consequences of our own. When a child steals his sister's candy, we might make him use his allowance to buy her new candy. Logical consequences are more effective than arbitrary consequences, because the child can see a cause-and-effect relationship between his actions and what happens next.

• Spankings

There's plenty of debate on the efficacy and appropriateness of spankings.* There are two schools of thought. Some experts say that spanking doesn't do anything to guide a child's internal motivation, that he behaves in order to avoid a spanking (or misbehaves, expecting and receiving a spanking, then misbehaves again—and again) without really thinking about his behavior, and that spanking teaches that violence is an okay way to handle tough situations. Others say that a little appropriate pain is an effective and valid way to reinforce limits.

One thing is for sure: There's a right way and a wrong way to spank. Impulsive spanking is ineffective—you'll likely find yourself offering little swats all day long, which gets you nowhere. Likewise, spanking should never, ever be a release for your anger.[8]

Dr. James Dobson says that spankings should be infrequent, used only when a child has willfully disobeyed. A spanking shouldn't occur when a child does something he didn't know was wrong; only spank if you have clearly communicated to your children what you expect of them, and they disobey in an act of deliberate defiance.[9]

---

*The editor does not endorse spanking in any form; however, he and the author feel it is important differing viewpoints are presented so the reader can choose the appropriate course of action for his or her family.

Remember that kids learn through repetition, and sometimes kids do something you've told them not to do simply because they forgot, so make a distinction between defiance and irresponsibility.

Dr. Dobson also believes that a spanking should be administered with "a neutral object," like a switch or belt, not the hand, and that spankings should occur immediately after misbehavior. And when the spanking is over, a child should be hugged and reassured of your love.

Something else to consider is that if other aspects of our parenting are out of alignment—if we're not spending enough time with our kids or showing them enough affection, or if parents are not a united front when it comes to discipline—spanking may exacerbate those problems.

- Time-Out

We all know the time-out. Some parents swear by them, others are exasperated by them, some experts love them, and some experts say they're effective only as a way to get kids to calm down. But for day-to-day offenses, a time-out may be just what the doctor ordered.

There are several keys to a successful time-out. The first step is to choose a place for the time-out, and it's important that we choose someplace boring and remove all dangerous, breakable, or valuable objects from the room. Laundry rooms or bathrooms are great. You'll also need to decide on how long to keep a child in time-out. Dr. Sal Severe recommends one or two minutes for toddlers, two or three minutes for preschoolers, and five minutes for kids five and older.[10] Finally, make sure your kids know the rules of time-out, explaining that when they do something they know they're not supposed to do, they'll have to go to the bathroom and sit quietly for five minutes. You'll set a timer, and they can come out when the timer goes off.

When you put a child in time-out, be sure to explain what's going on. Define the problem behavior in concrete terms: "You're arguing. Go to time-out." Try not to use descriptive words like *rude* or *obnoxious*; rather, be as specific as possible.

Be careful not to use a time-out for absolutely every little infraction, or they'll lose their effectiveness. For those smaller misbehaviors, simply redirect your kids or pull them out of the situation.

A Final Word

Discipline is hard work, and there will be times you simply fail. You'll probably lose your temper or give in or let your emotions get the better of you. But hang in there. You make your child's world a better place when you offer him the safety of boundaries and cultivate his ability to control himself.

CASE STUDY:

Making threats without following through doesn't work.

Bryan told his twelve-year-old son that he had to clean up his room or he would be grounded. But by the end of the week, the room was still not clean, and so Bryan had to put a moratorium on all activities for a set period of time. Unfortunately, the punishment happened to fall on the weekend of a father-son bike hike sponsored by their church.

"I was really looking forward to that trip," Bryan said. "I was tempted to just cancel his grounding—I mean, what a great activity. But I had backed down before, and he'd immediately slipped into old patterns. So I held my ground. I don't know who it hurt more, him or me. But I did notice a definite change in Joey's behavior—for the better. And we found another time to do our hike."

PERSONAL REFLECTION:

How do you think you're doing in terms of discipline? Do you ever feel like your kids are out of control, or have the feeling that you spent the whole day yelling? What area is a particular struggle for you?

✓ YOUR TO DO LIST:

Implement a two-week experiment with positive affirmation. Write down two behaviors you'd like to encourage in each child, and two you'd like to discourage. For the next two weeks, affirm and praise your kids when you catch them doing the two things on your "encourage" list, and affirm and praise them when they do the opposite of the things on your "discourage" list. At the end of two weeks, write out the improvements you see.

FOR FURTHER STUDY:

The Strong-Willed Child
—by Dr. James Dobson

CHAPTER 9

Establishing a Family Identity

When you look at your life, the greatest happinesses are family happinesses.

—JOYCE BROTHERS

POWER STATEMENT:

Creating a strong sense of your family's identity involves pursuing both unity and diversity and making each child feel like he or she belongs.

Y ou've been there. You start the day scrambling, hustle through work, then come home and hustle to get three kids to three ball practices on three different sides of town, grabbing dinner somewhere in between. Then it's homework, after which everyone collapses into bed, and then you get up in the morning and do it all again. And in all the chaos, you start to wonder if your kids feel that they belong in your family as strongly as they feel they belong on their basketball team.

Developing a strong sense of family identity is valuable for a lot of reasons. The feeling that they know and are known by their parents and siblings and belong to something important and stable contributes much to a child's sense of security. No matter how many times he rolls his eyes or how nerdy your kid may seem to think his family is, he really does appreciate having a place to belong when the world is harsh. Plus, a strong family identity will help a child resist negative outside influences and is a great way to pass along values and traditions that mean a lot to you.

And the good news is that creating a sense of family belonging is not hard at all, and it's probably one of the most fun things about parenting.

Family Unity in the Day-to-Day

By establishing a family identity, you're not trying to tell the world, "We are all like this," but rather, you're trying to tell your children, "You belong here." A family identity doesn't mean we're all exactly the same; it just means we're a united team, a group of people who care about each other and help each other along. As important as it is for a family to be unified, it's also important for our kids to feel that they can be themselves and that they have the freedom to change and grow as they get older.

For those reasons, when we set out to create a family identity, we'll do well to foster unity and diversity, making each child feel like an integral and unique part of the family.

The first step to family unity is to establish each child's position in the family. Nicknames are a great tool, particularly nicknames that express the child's personality. You might also think about a special handshake for each child, and of course, having one-on-one time with each child is so, so valuable and important.

You can also cultivate a sense of belonging by the way you set up your home. Photos and photo albums are a great tool, and they don't have to be an expensive or time-consuming project. A collage of photos captioned "The Myers Family" and portraying each family member's interests and personality can be displayed prominently but simply, reminding all of you that you're part of a unique family. Better yet—get your kids in on the act, and make an art project out of displaying family pictures.

It's also helpful to set your family space apart. Try to avoid making your living room the "catch-all" room, but rather, take steps to make that room say, "This is where we all spend time together." Stock the room with games and your favorite family DVDs and display photos of each family member. Find a way to display each family member's name—on pillows, picture frames, or other knick-knacks.

There are lots of other little ways to instill family pride. Make plays on your name—"The Tough McDuffs"—and look for ways to incorporate the wordplay in the day-to-day, like having a vanity license plate made, or titling the family's wall calendar, "The Tough McDuffs' Itinerary." And some of the best family unifiers aren't so serious: cheering for a favorite team together, listening to bluegrass or jazz together, or watching a favorite TV show.

As you use a few little day-to-day things to tell your kids, "We are a family," it's also important to let them know what kind of family you are. It's great to do things together, like hiking or fishing or basketball. The danger, though, in defining your family as an outdoorsy or athletic or bookish family is that if one member isn't outdoorsy or athletic or bookish, she might feel left out. You'll probably never please everyone, but it's important to make efforts to make sure everyone feels included at least some of the time—if Caitlin likes family volleyball games, but Jordan would rather stay in and watch a movie, plan a Saturday of volleyball one week, and rent a movie the next.

Plus, a solid family identity is based on values as much as hobbies and activities. You might say things like, "This family treats people with respect," when admonishing your eight-year-old for teasing another child. You might also plan family service projects, like spending a Saturday at a clothing closet or food pantry.

Another wonderful way to create a sense of family identity is to involve your extended family. Provide a time when your parents can tell your kids their life stories, or display pictures of great-grandparents and tell your kids about their lives. Every family has a heritage and a history, and even if they don't seem especially enthralled with the stories now, one day your kids will be glad they know where they come from.

A Rich Tradition

Here a few additional ideas sure to make your kids feel special and your home feel like home.

• Special Days

The Watkins family, though their patriarch is only approximately one-ninety-sixth Irish, nonetheless love celebrating St. Patrick's Day. On the morning of each March 17, mom Sharon assembles a small black container filled with gold-wrapped chocolates—pots of gold—for each family member, setting them out on the dining room table. That evening, the kids munch on candy as Sharon prepares a semi-authentic Irish feast of corned beef, cabbage, and soda bread, to be eaten with Celtic music playing in the background.

Holiday traditions are a great opportunity for family togetherness. We all have favorites, some of which seem a little silly to outsiders. And as discussed in Chapter 4, holidays are a wonderful time to pass on traditions of faith and to teach very tangible lessons, and they're guaranteed memory-makers. Besides that, they're just fun.

And of course, there's no law that says you can't have a special tradition that's not connected to a holiday. You might plan an annual zoo trip the week before school starts, or go bowling after the first school term. Whether it's yearly, monthly, or weekly, any fun activity or little tradition you implement with consistency will stay in your children's memories forever and solidify their sense of family.

• Birthdays

Particularly as kids get older, we feel a little pressured to make their birthdays a blowout to remember. But the truth is that our kids' most treasured birthday celebrations are the simplest ones—a special breakfast in bed and a handmade banner mean a lot more than balloon animals and thirty kids she hardly knows.

The key to making a birthday an opportunity to make a child feel like she belongs is to make it personal. Letters are wonderful, as are "the year in review" scrapbooks. Get the whole family in on it—each member's birthday should be a family holiday.

- Family Trips

They say you never really know someone until you travel with him. Family trips offer you concentrated time together and an opportunity to really get to know each other. Of course, when your kids get to be teens, they'll loathe being stuck in close quarters with their family—but not nearly as much as they let on.

And a family trip need not be expensive. There are some real advantages to traveling to local areas. For one thing, weekend trips are cheaper. For another thing, exploring local areas are a fun way to reinforce your kids' knowledge of their roots. As an eleven-year-old, Jenny didn't quite know what to think about her family's trip to a park full of life-sized concrete and fiberglass dinosaurs in eastern Arkansas. But as a thirty-year-old, she remembers how much her little brother loved dinosaurs and reflects fondly on a simple mini-vacation in Middle America.

• Coming-of-Age Ceremonies

Everyone loves a coming-of-age story—but no one loves being the main character in a coming-of-age story. And whatever your parents chose to do to commemorate your thirteenth birthday, you probably found it agonizingly embarrassing. Nonetheless, when your kids reach thirteen, fifteen, sixteen, or get their first apartment, it's time to celebrate, and making a fuss over them will help them know where they are on the map to adulthood. Plus, it gives your younger kids something to look forward to—or dread.

You might consider making a video for your new young adult, including interviews with special people in her life that let

DID YOU KNOW?

In Latin American cultures, a girl's fifteenth birthday is a big to-do, a commemoration of her entrance into adulthood and a celebration of tradition. The quinceañera (a title that refers to both the event and the birthday girl) celebration begins with a Misa de acción de gracias (thanksgiving Mass), during which the quinceañera wears a full-length white or light pink gown and is attended by a court consisting of her friends. The mass is followed by a banquet and lots of music and dancing.

her know how proud everyone is of her. You know better than anyone what will be meaningful to your child—funny presents, goofy ceremonies, or a more formal affair. And what best passes a torch on to your teen may be something less overt, like letting him do something by himself for the first time.

PERSONAL REFLECTION:

When you were growing up, what did your family do together? What was it about your life that made you feel like you were part of a family? Do you think your family feels like a team? What would you like to be different?

YOUR TO DO LIST:

Get started on your birthday plans today. The earlier you start, the more time you'll have to think about it, and the less stressed you'll be. Decide what you'd like to do for each child's birthday and start on a special letter to each of them.

FOR FURTHER STUDY:

Family Traditions: Practical, Intentional Ways to Strengthen Your Family Identity
        —by J. Otis Ledbetter and Tim Smith

CHAPTER 10

Educational Choices from Birth to College

Education is a shared commitment between dedicated teachers, motivated students and enthusiastic parents with high expectations.

—BOB BEAUPREZ

POWER STATEMENT:

There's no such thing as a perfect school, and once we've made the educational choice that best suits our kids' needs, it's up to us to take steps to maximize their education.

Education is serious business. Sometimes we feel pressured—choosing the right preschool, choosing between the now many options for elementary and secondary education, and let's not even talk about college. Everyone has an opinion about how we should be educating our kids, and no one wants to give our kids the right education as much as we do.

So before we even start to fill out enrollment papers and applications, we're wise to take a breather and decide what's most important to us. Are we most concerned that our kids be able to follow their dreams after high school? What do we most want them to learn—which academic arenas, and which life skills?

We should remember that sometimes the dreams we dream for our kids just aren't the dreams they dream for themselves—we may be concerned that our eighth-grader's school isn't getting her the test scores she needs to get into law school, while she has her heart set on being a teacher. We should also remember that as important as schooling is, there's no substitute for parents as a teacher of life skills.

Before They Go to School

You're your child's first and best teacher, and you can start getting them ready for school long before you pick out their first-day-of-kindergarten outfit.

A good place to start is to take measures to minimize your child's feelings of separation anxiety. School can be intimidating for a little kid, and it's helpful to get your child ready to be away from home. This is best accomplished early on by developing a close attachment with your baby—babies who are "securely attached" feel free to explore their environment, and they can handle it when their mother or father leaves for a short period of time. As your kids start walking, you can prepare them for a school day by making sure they have a chance to be around other adults. Leave them with your parents for a few hours at a time, or join a play group where they can interact with other kids and parents.

It's good to make sure your kids know how to be around other kids—they need to understand the value of taking turns and sharing. Give them opportunities to "practice" being with other kids. You shouldn't have a difficult time getting a friend to let you baby-sit her kids for a few hours on a Saturday.

Getting kids ready socially is one part of getting them ready for school. But an equally fun part is laying some groundwork for learning. The best way to do that is to familiarize them with language, which, again, starts when they're babies. Read books, even to your six-month-old, and let them get familiar with holding a book and turning the pages.

It's extremely valuable to simply talk to your babies and toddlers. Be interactive—when reading a book, ask them about the pictures or the story: "What does that monkey have on his head?" A child's brain is most plastic between the ages of zero and five, so take advantage of these years.

Be careful to be relaxed about your educational efforts. Reading books should be fun, not forced. Keeping things light will ensure that your kids see reading and learning as something they can enjoy, not something boring and regimented.

At some point, you'll be ready to think about preschool. You do have some options. The current trend at many public schools is to extend kindergarten to a full day and offer a four-year-old program, and there are also Head Start-type programs available in many areas. And of course there are private preschools, some of which are very specially designed.

But not every child needs to attend preschool, and it's up to you to decide whether your child is ready to spend half a day in a structured setting. A non-preschool childhood is easily supplemented by taking special field trips and helping your little one explore the world around him—and continuing to read together—which is a great thing to do even if your child does attend preschool.

One way or another, kindergarten teachers love it when

kids have been prepared for school, and preschool is a great way to do that. If you do decide to enroll your child in preschool, you'll need to make sure she's potty trained, and talk to her about preschool, letting her know what to expect.

K-12

Education is always a little bit of a hot topic, whether it's in the political arena or in the church parking lot. There's something about preparing a child to face the future that lends itself to lots of strong feelings.

These days, we have a lot (a *lot*) of options for elementary and secondary schools, and there's just no such thing as a perfect school. The key is to determine your child's needs and figure out which schooling option is the best fit. And don't forget to talk to your kids—find out what they like and dislike about school, what they most want in a school.

But whatever schooling option we choose, the only way to take full advantage of it is to take responsibility for our kids' academic and emotional development, getting involved, knowing what our kids are learning and doing, and supplementing our kids' educational lives as needed.

Here's a brief rundown of the most prevalent options, as well as a few thoughts on whether they might be right for you.

● Public Schools

The good:

In terms of bare practicality, public schools are free, and transportation is usually very easily arranged. Public schools also offer a wide variety of activities and services—sports teams, career counselors, and the like. Plus, it's not hard to see that public schools are full of teachers and principals who accept little pay in exchange for the rewards of teaching. Public schools are simply not short on educators who truly care about kids and want them to excel.

The bad:

Public schools are much criticized in terms of offering an effective education. They are very often underfunded, and sometimes underproductive. In all fairness, public schools are at the mercy of the standardized test system, which is a somewhat questionable way to measure whether students are really learning.

Something else you'll need to consider is the potential clash of ideology between your kids and their teachers and curriculum—and sometimes other students. Some parents are fearful of what their kids might be exposed to in public schools in terms of worldview and lifestyle issues.

Cost:

None, except for school supplies.

Public schools are the prevailing choice, it seems, and for good reason—public schools are free and close, no small issues for any parent.

There's plenty of talk these days concerning school choice—lots of people want to make it possible for parents to send their kids to the school of their choice within their district, or even within their state. The onus is on us to evaluate the schools in our district and determine where our kids should go, and we can get the information we need by simply calling the superintendent's office or meeting with the principal. It's important to look at these items (which you should do for any school you're examining as a choice for your child):

- How many years of experience the teachers have.
- What sports and activities are offered.
- The average class size.
- The rate of students who stay on until graduation.[1]

You might also ask about gifted programs, advanced placement, and honors programs if your child is above average.

There are ways to maximize your child's public school education. The chief way to do this is to get involved. Volunteer. Make use of parent-teacher conferences and ask lots of questions. Stay in touch with your kids and know what goes on at school. And if you're worried about their social lives or the potential negative influence of other students, take steps to nurture your child's social life. The truth is that the success of any schooling option depends on our being engaged and involved in our child's life and education.

- Charter Schools

The good:

Charter schools tend to be smaller than other public schools, which can be a real advantage. A charter school is very often self-governing and very community-oriented, hiring their own teachers and creating their own curriculum and teaching methods. For this reason, charter schools usually involve their teachers to a greater degree, as well as parents.

Charter schools are sometimes seen as something of a savior for inner city schools, providing an alternative for students who live in an underperforming school district. Evaluating the truth of that belief isn't really an open-and-shut case, but charter schools do offer a very engaged, deliberate approach to education, which may be a major improvement over the public school in your district.

The bad:

Proximity can be an issue—since charter schools aren't particularly common, it may not be easy to find one in your area. Also, many charter schools are fairly new, which makes them a little harder to evaluate, and they often struggle for a few years before establishing academic strength.[2] Plus, with charter schools being so new and somewhat sparse, there are waiting lists nationwide to get into these schools.

Cost:

Since they're state-funded, charter schools are free, though some charter schools require uniforms.

Charter schools vary from state to state, but they're basically semi-autonomous public schools. Some operate on a contract with the local school district, but as a rule charter schools are free from many of the regulations that apply to other public schools. Many charter schools are formed to serve a special population or fulfill a certain educational vision, which may be just what you're looking for. Something to keep in mind is that a lot of charter schools expect a certain level of parent involvement, and it's wise to find out how many hours a month a charter school would ask of you in determining if that school is right for you.

• Private Schools

The good:

Private schools are varied, and you're probably most interested in private schooling for your kids if you're interested in a particular ideology or religious approach, or if you're looking for a school with a solid academic reputation—the "college prep" aspect of private schooling. Visit most private schools, and you'll likely experience a vibrant, optimistic feel and meet teachers and administrators who take education very seriously.

The bad:

Most private schools use an application process. And some private schools don't offer bus service, which means you'll have to think about transportation.

Cost:

Can be substantial. According to the National Association of Independent schools, the median annual tuition for private day schools for elementary schools is $12,000; for middle schools, that number is $13,000, and $15,000 for high schools.

Private schools come in a rainbow of educational approaches and ideologies. Fortunately, private schools don't make it too hard for you to learn about their mission and approach. You can learn more about any private school that interests you usually on the Web or by asking for a brochure or meeting with the principal. Find out how long the school has been in existence, and ask about the four points suggested above for evaluating public schools. Remember that it's not a given that any particular private school is academically thriving.

If you're worried that your teen or preteen might be making or start making some wrong choices, you may be looking into private school in order to keep her on the straight and narrow, thinking that a school full of students whose parents want them to be there will be a better environment for your child. You may be right, but keep in mind that other parents may be sending their kids to that school in order to straighten them out. In other words, if your child is determined to find bad friends, he'll probably find them wherever he goes. The best prevention against bad choices is *you*.

- Home Schooling

The good:

Home schooling provides much more individual attention than most other schooling options, which might be just what your child needs. Transportation is virtually a non-issue. As with private schools, you're probably most interested in home schooling if you're concerned about the philosophy behind the educational institutions available to you. Home schooling allows you to decide how your children will be taught about sensitive issues.

Home schooling isn't as hard as it may seem. There is a process to follow (and some states are more accommodating than others), but it's fairly easy to get started. And you're probably more qualified than you think—you were your child's first teacher, after all, and there are lots of avenues available to assist you in teaching well.

The bad:

Obviously, home schooling is going to require a big time investment and simply may not be an option for families with working parents (not that all parents

HOW TO START HOME SCHOOLING:

• A good place to start is by contacting a local home schooling group and asking for information. They can let you know what your state requirements are.

• Contact the state to find out what your state's recordkeeping laws are—some are detailed, some have virtually none. You'll also need to find out if your state requires a declaration of intent, which might be a form or a simple, signed letter that states that you intend to home school your kids.

• Determine how you'll go about finding a curriculum. You can buy materials or create your own. You don't have to go it alone—there are lots of groups and co-ops you can work with.

aren't working!). Some home school advocates swear you can work and home school, but that would inevitably require some special handling. Another obstacle, albeit a minor one, is that there is a certain process to go through in order to start homeschooling.

A lot of people are quick to point out that home-schooled kids may be slightly stunted socially, and your family will probably have to work at exposing your kids to unfamiliar situations and nurturing their social skills. Home school groups and co-ops offer lots of assistance and ideas, and some local school districts even allow home-schooled children to take one class a day or week or participate on sports teams.

Cost:

Most curriculums are fairly inexpensive; you might expect to pay about $500 a year. And it's entirely conceivable that you might be able to create a curriculum for free.

Your child may really need home schooling—if she needs a little more help or a little less structure, home schooling might be right up her alley. You will have to do some thinking about whether your family is ready to have school in the living room. If you have small children as well as school-age children, it may not be so easy to structure your day, not to mention prepare lesson plans. It's certainly not impossible—lots of people do it—but you'll need to take some time to figure out if home schooling is feasible for your family.

After High School

You've made thirteen years of schooling decisions—and now it's time to make another one, a big one. Post-high-school schooling can be a huge stressor for you and your teen. But you can minimize the stress and strain by working together.

This should be largely your teen's decision, with you acting as advisor. Make this fun—have an early brainstorming session over lunch at a favorite restaurant sometime during your kid's junior year. You'll probably encounter your share of disagreements, but do your best to work through them and focus on the goal at hand: finding the campus that will best launch your pre-freshman into adulthood.

Phase one is to take stock of your teen's strengths and interests. What are her preliminary career goals? What subject areas does he most enjoy? What are her favorite extracurricular activities?

While you're thinking and dreaming, remember that academics and careers are only part of the equation. What are your teen's larger needs? Is she looking for a close-knit college with a strong sense of community? Is diversity in a college a particular issue for your student? Does he want or need to be close to home? Does she need to make some particular strides toward independence?

Not everyone needs to go to college, and some students benefit greatly from spending a couple years at a community college before moving on. What's important is that your grad conquers the challenges that will give him the confidence he needs to move into the future.

If your student is college bound, once you've outlined some goals, it's time for her to look at colleges with an eye toward which ones will best help her meet those goals. There is no shortage of information available—colleges want you to find them. Your student can go to college fairs, talk to guidance counselors, search the Web. Have him highlight the schools that appeal to him.

Once you've gotten an idea of which schools your teen is most open to, one idea is to start college binder, with a section for each of the schools that most appeal to your teen (it's probably good to keep it down to four or five). Print each school's vitals from their webpage and file them in the binder.

Next, start evaluating each school. Check out their academic and financial requirements. Do your student's grades and test scores qualify them for admission and/or scholarships? How expensive are the schools he's

CASE STUDY:

Ken and Gloria have three kids, one in public school, one in a private Christian school, and one home schooled.

"We learned the hard way, at least for our family, that one size doesn't fit all," said Gloria. "We started off planning to home school all three. We could see with our oldest daughter, who is very social and a great athlete, she was just so much happier in a setting where she could be a team member. We worried that she wouldn't have our values, but that's not the case. And then with our middle son, we found that he did much better in a more structured environment, and he loves his school. So now we've got three happy students, and even though it's a challenge to keep up with all their school activities, I wouldn't have it any other way."

interested in, and are they financially feasible? Evaluate the quality of the school according to your priority criteria: academics, diversity, or athletics. At this point, your student may be ready to eliminate a school or two from his list.

A campus visit is extremely helpful. Call ahead and schedule a time when your teen can visit and meet with admissions counselors, professors and coaches, and other students. It's helpful to stay overnight so that she can get a feel for campus life. Advise her to be a sponge—asking questions, reading bulletin boards, and observing what goes on around campus.

Eventually, your teen will have to make a decision based on courses of study, financial and academic considerations, and overall appeal. All that's left for you to do is try not to burst into tears at graduation.

PERSONAL REFLECTION:

What did you most appreciate about your education? What did you experience that you'd like to shield your kids from?

✓ YOUR TO DO LIST:

If your kids are in school, take a minute today to analyze your current education situation. Get your kids in on it—ask them what they like and don't like about school. What needs to change? Is it something you can work through, or do you need to consider changing schools?

FOR FURTHER STUDY:

The New Public School Parent
    —by Bob Chase with Bob Katz

Getting the Best Education for Your Child
    —by James Keogh

www.greatschools.net

CHAPTER 11

Health, Sports, and Nutrition

To insure good health: eat lightly, breathe deeply, live moderately, cultivate cheerfulness, and maintain an interest in life.

—WILLIAM LONDEN

POWER STATEMENT:

A healthy lifestyle is all about balance: balanced nutrients, balanced amounts of exercise and rest, and a balanced attitude.

We live in a fairly health-conscious society. The latest medical findings on the value of blueberries or salmon or Froot Loops are ever before us. Diet and weight loss books consistently top bestsellers lists. And yet, according to plenty of statistics, Americans aren't especially healthy.

Kids are not immune from the health obsession, and as many different voices are telling them how to be healthy, none of them are as important as you.

Preventative Medicine: Nutrition and Health

We all think about food—a lot. You may make less-than-healthy choices, then feel bad about it, or spend what seems like all your time and energy trying to eat healthy. When we have kids, it's no different. We worry about how they're eating—or maybe in our own lives, we closely associate food and weight with being beautiful and don't want to burden our kids with that pressure, so we don't manage their eating too closely. It doesn't help that we're constantly on the go, and convenient "kid" foods aren't really all that healthy.

It does matter how our kids eat—a balanced diet can give them an edge in their academic and athletic success—but just as important is our healthy, balanced attitude. A child won't die because he eats chicken fingers and French fries. And our relaxed attitude about food will help make mealtime a relatively stress-free event, which makes it more likely that kids will eat the foods they need.

Here are some basic principles for good eating.

Before your kids are weaned, food choices are a bit of a no-brainer—it's just a matter of choosing between breast-feeding and bottles. If you do breastfeed, remember to keep up your strength by snacking on healthy things like fresh and dried fruit, granola bars, and nuts (not that an Oreo or three ever hurt anyone), and drinking lots of water.[1]

Things get a little more complicated when it's time to start introducing solid food. Work very, very closely with your pediatrician in determining when to start introducing solid foods and what foods to start out on. There are lots of differing

DID YOU KNOW?

Heating milk or formula in the microwave can break down certain nutrients and heat unevenly. It's best to warm bottles in a pot of warm water.

opinions, but conventional wisdom is to start your six-month-old baby out on rice cereals (not wheat-based or oatmeal cereals, due to the possibility of food allergies) and then move on to vegetables and fruits, and remember that breast milk or formula should still be your baby's main source of nutrients. The American Dietetic Association encourages parents to make a variety fruits and vegetables available to older babies and toddlers, aiming for five a day without forcing anything past your baby's appetite.

Once your kids are full-fledge eaters of solid food, your main goal is to make food choices that meet their nutritional needs. Kids, just like adults, have some larger nutritional needs (macronutrients) and smaller ones (micronutrients). The big ones, the "macronutrients," are protein (meat, dairy, beans, and nuts), fat (oils and animal fats), and carbohydrates (pastas, breads, cereals, potatoes, and rice). You probably remember all of these from health class. Proteins are your body's building blocks, fats aid in cell function, and carbohydrates give the body energy, to put it simply. The micronutrients your child needs are vitamins and minerals, which serve a variety of functions, including regulating the body's enzymes, hormones, and metabolism. And of course, there's water, and your kids should get five to eight glasses of water a day, a little more if they're particularly active in sports.

As a guideline for how much of what to give your kids, there's the food pyramid: four servings of cereals and grains, four or more of vegetables and fruits, three of meat (or any solid source of protein like eggs, dried beans, or peanut butter), and four a day of milk and cheese. At the top of the pyramid are fats and sweets, which are to be used sparingly.

Easier said than done. Here are a few ideas on making meals healthy:

- It's tough to get all the veggies and fruits your kids need into a day. You might have to get creative. You could try grating vegetables where they might not otherwise be found, like pizza or spaghetti sauce. If you have smaller kids, make it fun—make a veggie art project out of pitas and various chopped or shredded veggies and cheese. And, if all else fails, there's always the smoothie.

- Preparation will be your friend, especially if you're an always-on-the-go family. Plan ahead and stock your pantry with lots of basics: tortillas, pitas, lunch meat, cottage cheese, oatmeal and cereal. Minced garlic is a wonder, as are frozen fruits and veggies. You can prepare snacks in advance by freezing single servings of grapes or berries to be tucked into a lunchbox or gym bag.

- Takeout is probably a staple for your family. Try to keep fast food to a minimum. Lots of your favorite (though more expensive) sit-down restaurants offer takeout menus; you can call ahead and pick up the food on your way to or from practice, church, or home.

If you have a picky eater, you're probably a little battle weary—particularly if you've ever even thought about serving green beans. There are ways to get healthy foods into the tummies of picky eaters. You might look for ways to make food fun, especially if your kids are little, like dipping fruits or vegetables into yogurt, guacamole, peanut butter, or cottage cheese. You might also have success by inviting over for dinner a slightly older child who loves to eat, to serve as kind of a role model. There's always the "bite system": "Take two bites of chicken and one bite of squash." The reality is that some kids—and adults—are simply picky, and you may have to find creative recipes to build on their few favorites.

Of course, there's more to being healthy than just eating well. Getting exercise is vital to kids' cardiovascular fitness, muscle and bone development, and overall health.

The best—and most fun—approach to kids' fitness is to make it a family affair. Shoot hoops together. Take walks. Plan Saturday hiking trips. Try to keep up a good frequency—the Centers for Disease Control are urging kids to spend some time being active every day.

But another important aspect of kids' health is to get some rest. According to psychologist Peter Sheras, kids need unstructured time to regroup and recuperate from the things that fill up their days.[2]

Kids do need to eat well and learn to take good care of themselves. But we also need to be careful about the emphasis we put on food and dieting.

Kids are bombarded with messages about health and beauty all day long—they may feel urged by school officials, friends, parents, and media images to avoid being fat at all costs. They may not realize that thinness does not always equal health, and if kids reject good nutrition in an effort to lose weight, they're actually doing their bodies a serious disservice. Plus, it's unhealthy for any child or adult to be obsessed with food and weight—there's a reason the term "body image" gets thrown around so much in schools and parenting magazines.

The best thing you can do is to model a healthy attitude toward food and body image. Take time to assess your relationship with food—do you find yourself feeling guilty (and expressing feelings of guilt) for what you eat? Do you judge your physical appearance fairly?

As you adopt a healthy attitude toward dieting, you'll develop a healthy attitude toward food, which will wear off on your kids. The goal: viewing food as fuel for life to be used and enjoyed.

Healthy Bodies, Healthy Minds: Helping Your Child Succeed in Sports

Sports can be an extremely valuable experience for kids. Being active in sports has long been credited with keeping kids away from negative choices. Playing sports helps your child get the exercise he needs and can build his sense of belonging. Plus, organized (or at least semi-organized) sports are a great teaching tool—there are things your kid can learn by playing on a team that you could never teach just by talking: doing your best, sticking to it, handling disappointment, teamwork.

Sports can also do a lot for your child's self-esteem. As we talked about in Chapter 6, kids need to achieve in order to earn self-esteem, and sports can help them do that. So be careful about shielding your player from competition. If he's not doing well, make sure you help him find other avenues to excel, and use your discretion to determine if he should stick out the season, keeping in mind that quitting can be an even bigger self-esteem sabotage than losing. Let your child know she doesn't have to win for you to be proud of her.

It's helpful for us to remember that our kids' sports are their thing. It makes kids feel important and secure when we get involved with them and their interests, and we should be loving, enthusiastic spectators and supporters. But especially for older kids, it's important to give them room to take ownership. And if we find ourselves getting a little too emotional at the games—or putting a little too much emphasis on winning—we need to realign our priorities and make sure we're not putting too much pressure on our players.

If you've caught yourself getting a little hot under the collar, make sure you model good sportsmanship for your kids. Be careful not to blame others for your child's mistakes in an effort to make him feel better—it will ultimately backfire. Even if the umpires, refs, or coaches made glaring mistakes, don't bad-mouth them. Holding your tongue will teach your child to be gracious and take responsibility for his own actions.

After each loss, look for the positive: "You really played your heart out. I'm proud of you." (But never affirm your child's behavior if to do so is untrue!) Or, "I can really tell you've worked on your form," or "You seem to have a lot more endurance than you used to."

If all else fails, a mantra may be in order: "Sports should be *fun*. Sports should be *fun*. Sports should be *fun*."

When Your Child Gets Sick

It's scary when a child gets sick, and we've all made our share of calls to Mom when our babies got the sniffles. It's not easy, but keeping a clear head will help us make good decisions when our kids get sick.

The first question we encounter when one of our kids catches a bug is whether or not we should call a doctor. Most pediatricians advise parents to err on the side of caution—call the office, and let the doctor make a judgment on whether or not to bring your child in. As a rule of thumb, if your child is six weeks old or younger and has a fever of 100.4 degrees or greater, call a physician immediately. You should also call the doctor's office if your child has been vomiting for six hours and seems unable to keep anything down; if a fever lasts for longer than twenty-four hours (act more quickly if your baby is three months old or younger); or if your child exhibits difficulty breathing, extreme lethargy, or confusion.

But lots of times, our kids catch bugs that aren't so serious. If your child has a fever, you can offer fever reducers like acetaminophen and ibuprofen and generally make him comfortable with cool compresses and drinks. For vomiting, offer clear liquids to keep your child hydrated. If she's able to keep these down, offer food a few hours after the last vomiting spell, something bland like crackers, soup, or potatoes.

> **FAST FACT:**
>
> According to Reuters, one study showed that alternating between acetaminophen and ibuprofen is more effective than using only one of the two for bringing down a fever in young kids.

You remember the ways your parents took care of you when you were sick as a kid. There's a lot to be said for conventional wisdom—and lots of comfort.

The point of having a healthy body is to be able to enjoy life to the fullest. So if at any time your efforts to keep your family healthy lead to increased stress or major family feuds, don't abandon your efforts altogether, but back off and reevaluate. Make efforts to build healthy habits into your family's everyday life, putting the emphasis on healthy relationships and a healthy lifestyle. In the words of the Bible, "Life is more than food, the body more than clothes."

CASE STUDY:

"It wasn't until I saw our family picture from vacation at the beach," said Wendy, "that I realized I didn't recognize our smiling faces anymore. Bob and I were now quite heavy, which I could almost live with and accept, but when I saw how heavy our kids were getting, I realized we had a problem.

"I withstood a new Civil War that included my husband, but I got rid of the sweets and packaged snacks and made fresh fruit and vegetables our snack food of choice. I saw a lot of apple slices turn brown and bananas go soft, but when that's what's on the counter after school and work—and there's no cookies in the cupboard—you get hungry enough to eat them!"

PERSONAL REFLECTION:

Do you find yourself worrying about your kids' health?
How do you think you're doing in terms of building and
modeling a healthy lifestyle? What would you change?

✓ YOUR TO DO LIST:

Implement a family activity session a couple evenings a
week. Play some basketball together or go for a walk. If you think
it's worth the investment, you might think about a subscription to
the Y to swim or shoot hoops during the seasons when it gets
dark early.

FOR FURTHER STUDY:

www.nutritionforkids.com

Eating
        —by Michelle Kennedy

*It's Just a Game! Youth, Sports, and Self-Esteem: A
Guide for Parents*
        —by Darrell Burnett, PhD.

*Parenting, SportsMom Style: Real-Life Solutions for
Surviving the Youth Sports Scene*
        —by Laurel Phillips and Barbara Stahl

Managing Family Conflict

If you have never been hated by your child, you have never been a parent.

—BETTE DAVIS

POWER STATEMENT:

The key to managing conflict is communication, communication, communication.

Unpleasant reality #1: Your family will have conflict. You can't live with and care about someone without occasionally disagreeing. Actually, if your family currently doesn't have any conflict, something's wrong. Unpleasant reality #2: It won't always be easy to defuse the situation. But ignoring the problem isn't an option—burying family conflict tends to make it worse and might even permanently damage a relationship.

The good news is that healthy conflict can make your family stronger as you communicate about the deeper issues of your family and reaffirm your love for each other.

Preventative Medicine

We can't avoid family feuds. But long before they start, we can take measures to defuse them and create a healthy family life.

The first step is the hardest. We need to begin with a little self-examination. What's your fighting style? Do you swallow your anger, then lash out later? Do you get personal? Do you avoid conflict altogether?

Even if it's a little hard to face, you probably know what you do in a conflict—you've probably seen the effects of your fighting style time and time again. No one is perfect, and your key to relational success is your willingness to take responsibility for your imperfections. No, not everything is your fault, and it's not healthy to take an unnatural responsibility for others' behavior. But if you're willing to do everything in your power to help you and your family work through the conflicts that come your way, you're in great shape.

Once we've applied a little preventative medicine to our own hearts, it's time to do some preemptive nurturing in our relationship with the other members of our family. Stephen R. Covey suggests looking at family life like a banking system, making sure to put plenty of "deposits" in others' accounts. Pick up dinner on your way home. Rent your son's favorite movie to watch together. Find out what communicates love to your spouse and kids and strategically show them that you love them. Those little kindnesses and courtesies will strengthen your relationship, helping ensure that you'll survive the next conflict.

Obviously, what won't work is doing lots of nice things for your spouse and kids to use as ammunition for your next battle—"How can you say that? After all I do for you…" Rather, your goal is to keep your interactions with your family loving.

Families require maintenance. With a little effort, we equip our families with the things we need to work through conflict: forgiveness, humility, and love.

Conflict Toolbox

When you do encounter conflict, it is possible to get past it—and grow from it. Here are a few tools for working through conflict.

The first tool is the airing of grievances—in the proper way. For one thing, timing is everything. It's not good to keep quiet about our complaints and store them up for a knock-down, drag-out. Or maybe you brush off the things that bother you with no intention of ever bringing them up—but somehow they manage to surface accompanied by more than a few angry words. When something bothers you, say so. It might be best to cool off for a while before bringing up your grievance, but don't wait too long.

As much as you want to do the talking when you're angry, the best thing you can do is listen. Don't assume you understand the other person's actions or perspective. If your daughter has been sassing you, let her know how you feel about it and then listen to her response. She may be feeling overwhelmed or lost in the shuffle or have a grievance with you that she needs to get off her chest. By listening to her, you reduce the chances the behavior will be repeated because you'll have addressed the root issues, whereas if you simply yell at her to stop, the problem may get worse.

In *Love and Anger*, Nancy Samalin suggests several

principles for expressing anger.[1] It's important, for example, to control our speech as much as possible, using "I" statements rather than the "you" statements that put the other person on the defensive: "I'm really feeling frustrated," rather than "You never pay attention to anything that goes on around here." It's also important, Samalin says, for us to stay in the present. Don't dredge up ancient history, and don't project the current problem into the future. Be short and to the point in airing your grievance. And once you've discussed the problem and worked out a solution, restore good feelings by reaffirming your love for the other person.

Knowing how to express your anger is a great tool for managing conflict. Another important item in your conflict-management toolbox is the family meeting. A regular family meeting serves so many purposes: It lends your family a sense of unity, solidarity, and identity, and it offers all of you a chance to solve problems before they get out of hand.

Keep your family meeting structured, but loosely. Once a month is great—some parents like to make it fun by delivering colorful reminder "invitations" to each kid the week of the meeting. You might also look for fun ways to keep order and make sure everyone talks in turn. One possibility is to select an object like a stuffed animal or a football and declare that no one is allowed to talk unless they're holding the object.

Use the time to talk about upcoming events, scheduling—and any problems that may need addressing. Encourage your kids to share, and if there's an issue that's particularly sensitive, a child may need to approach you about it privately before the meeting. A word of caution: The "sharing" aspect of a family meeting only works if you're nurturing your relationship with your kids between meetings in such a way that they feel they can bring up sensitive issues with you.

You want everyone to get a chance to talk at your family meeting. There are differing opinions on how democratic a family should be, but don't be afraid to negotiate. Showing flexibility isn't the exact same thing as showing weakness. Plus, when kids feel like they have a certain amount of say-so in their family life, they're more likely to take responsibility for the climate in your house. Try to strike that balance of being a compassionate and receptive, yet conscientious and firm parent.

It's all about communication. Taking the time and making the effort to communicate will make the difference between growing from conflict and allowing it to overtake your relationships.

Marriage Matters

As parents, your marriage matters. Your kids are

watching to see how you respond to conflict, and hostility between parents can warp a child's perception of relationships and take away from their sense of security in your family. Besides, you and your spouse need to present a united front to your kids in terms of discipline, which is so much easier when you're taking time to nurture your marriage.

How do we keep our marriage strong and (generally) happy? According to Susan Page, the happiest couples are characterized, among other things, by a willingness to facilitate goodwill. They resist blaming each other, focus on the positives, express gratitude to be together, and demonstrate a willingness to give.[2] Happy couples have somehow managed to hold onto that admiration and respect for each other they had when they first got married.

And that's something all of us can work toward. It's a matter of choosing how we think about our spouse, choosing to focus on their positives instead of their negatives. It's so easy to feel slighted, and there are always things we need to work through, but it is possible to choose to see our spouse in the best possible light.

Obviously, being happy together doesn't mean you never argue. It just means your conflicts are easier to work through—it's easier to be forgiving toward someone who's quick to express that they like you.

When you do argue, there's a right way and a wrong way to do it. Again, your kids are watching, and you have the opportunity to model healthy conflict resolution. Most experts advise couples to keep arguing out of view of the kids, and anytime you disagree on a disciplinary measure, you should probably discuss it out of earshot, but it's probably not necessary for kids to believe that Mom and Dad never disagree. Settle your grievances, following the suggestions listed above for expressing anger, before they pile up and threaten your marriage.

For most couples, it's when kids enter the picture that a marriage is most strained. Particularly once a brand-new baby comes home, the classic arguments ensue: too little sex, not enough attention, and not enough help around the house. It's important to settle these squabbles in a meaningful way, not just addressing the practical matters but restoring intimacy to your marriage. And you'll help yourselves out a lot by setting aside a regular time for just the two of you to reconnect. Again, families require maintenance, and marriages are no different.

If you're going it alone as a single parent, you have some very special challenges facing you. Your relationship with your kids' mother or father is most likely not remotely tidy or easy, and you probably face frustration on a daily basis. You'll do well to resist the urge to vent that frustration to your kids. And as difficult as it is to have to pick up the pieces when your former spouse disappoints the kids, do everything you can not to impede their relationship.

Once again, your kids are watching. They need to see their parents work at good relationships—even in less-than-ideal situations.

Sibling Wars

All siblings fight from time to time. But sometimes, a sibling war somehow manages to make life miserable for everyone in the house. The question that always comes to mind is, "Do I intervene?"

Sometimes they need to work it out on their own. But if they're on the verge of really hurting each other—verbally or physically—it's time to step in and end the feud. In *Siblings Without Rivalry*, authors Adele Faber and Elaine Mazlish suggest these four steps to intervening: 1) Acknowledge their anger. 2) Listen to each side. 3) Show appreciation for the difficulty of the problem. 4) Express faith that they can work it out and arrive at a fair solution. 5) Leave the room. If the war seems to escalate rather than dissipate, send them to separate corners to cool off, but don't express anger.[3]

In general, saying things like, "You guys are driving me crazy," probably isn't going to help the situation, and try your best not to show partiality.

The reality is that siblings just fight sometimes—toys, TV, music, bedrooms. But sometimes sibling anger can be a deep, potentially dangerous thing. Siblings fight because they're competing; your job is to figure out if they're competing for the front seat or for attention or love.

There are things you as a parent can do to minimize your kids' conflict. Spend regular one-on-one time with your kids, which has a way of making each child feel like a "favorite." And never, never complain about one of your kids to the others.

Parent-Child Conflict

Struggling in our relationship with our kids is no fun. It's not too bad to butt heads once in a while, but when arguing becomes the hallmark of the week, we're ready for retirement. There are some things we need to keep in mind when it comes to parent-child conflict.

For one thing, some conflict is necessary—and good. Kids need discipline, and discipline means focusing on our kids needs, not their wants. We're not our kids' friends; we're their parents.

This can be especially hard to remember when our kids get to be teens and we start to feel distant from them. Just remember those commercials where various young adults complained to their parents: "You asked me questions. You set curfews. I hated it… Thanks." There are times we have to get in our kids' faces, and that kind of conflict is good.

Obviously, that doesn't mean we're always right or that we can say anything we want. Respecting our kids is the only way they gain confidence to take responsibility of their own lives, and we need to follow the rules of good communication and listening.

Something else you may need to consider is that today's kids don't seem to fight authority so much as ignore authority. So if you're never in conflict with your teen, you may want to examine your relationship and make sure you're not two ships passing in the night, so to speak.

On the other hand, if you're constantly fighting with your child, something may be wrong, and it may not be you. The American Academy of Child and Adolescent Psychology lists these symptoms as possible indicators of Oppositional Defiant Disorder:

- Frequent tantrums
- Excessive arguing with adults
- Defiance and refusal to comply with adult directives
- Antisocial behavior, including a proclivity to deliberately annoy or upset others
- Blaming his mistakes or misbehavior on others

- Easily becoming upset or annoyed

- Hateful speech when angry

- Seeking revenge

If your child seems to be more difficult to manage than

Step by Step

One of the toughest adult-child conflicts occurs between kids and their new stepparents. It's tough for both parties to figure out exactly how this relationship is going to work, and sometimes kids, worried that they're no longer number-one in their biological parent's lives, can lash out at new stepmoms and stepdads.

Here are a few ideas from *Parenting* magazine on easing the transition.

- Be gracious. Kids may feel like they have to compete for their biological parent's attention. Help them feel more secure by allowing and encouraging your spouse to spend one-on-one time with his kids. (Likewise, make sure you get some one-on-one time with your spouse to help quell your feelings of being left out.)

- Go slow. Try to introduce changes slowly. Kids' lives should stay as much the same as possible, and give your new family a year before making any major changes in the way the household runs.

is developmentally or temperamentally reasonable, talk to your pediatrician and see about getting an evaluation. If the doctor determines that there might really be a problem, it might be wise to consider getting two or three opinions. This will help you know what you're dealing with and help you find the best doctor for your family's needs.

Living together means conflict. But conflict doesn't have to be a bad thing—butting heads is often how we learn something important about ourselves or others. So don't create conflict, but don't shy away from it, either.

PERSONAL REFLECTION:

Do you tend to avoid arguments or start them? Do you think you're basically a fair fighter? What's the chief source of conflict in your home.

☑ YOUR TO DO LIST:

Institute a monthly family meeting. Pick a time that works for everyone and send invitations to the family living room.

FOR FURTHER STUDY:

The Seven Habits of Highly Effective Families
  —by Stephen Covey

Siblings Without Rivalry
  —by Adele Faber and Elaine Mazlish

CHAPTER

Leading By Example

---

*It is easier to exemplify values
than teach them.*

—THEODORE HESBURGH

POWER STATEMENT:

Our kids learn from us best
when we teach them with a
combination of words and
actions.

We've talked about modeling throughout the preceding chapters. The truth is that the way we live is one of the most effective tools for shaping a child's behavior (and sometimes knowing that our kids are watching keeps us on the straight and narrow as well!).

There's an educational theory that states that learners absorb 25% of what they hear, 40% of what they see, and 70% of what is taught both verbally and by modeling. So it's really no surprise that we often find ourselves repeating what we say and that our kids respond much better to a combination of actions and words.

Why is modeling so effective? Because kids, consciously or not, often adopt our attitude toward people and situations. So when we model, we don't just teach our kids how to behave in certain situations, but how to think.

For one thing, our kids will likely adopt our attitude toward spiritual matters. If we want our kids to value church, we have to make church a priority in our family. If we want our kids to value prayer, we have to let our kids see us pray. When we model spiritual actions, we teach our kids to value spiritual things.

So the key to modeling, maybe especially when it comes to spiritual matters, is to make sure we combine our actions and our words. Charlie faithfully let his kids out of the car at the front door of the church each Sunday, and then went to get a cup of coffee and a paper. Later in life, he reached a point where he wanted to be in church and wanted his kids to want to be in church, but they resisted, particularly his oldest son. He found he was unable to teach his kids to value something that, for years, he didn't value himself—at least not enough to actually get himself through the church doors.

Modeling is an extremely effective way to teach all kinds of values. There's no way to make your kids be compassionate, but if you demonstrate compassion, you've done a lot toward instilling in them a compassionate heart. Buy Thanksgiving groceries for families in need and take your kids to the grocery store with you, or spend extra time talking to a friend who's upset. Likewise, you'll find it difficult to force your kids to have respect for their teachers and coaches, but if you respect your kids and spouse and let them see you act respectfully toward your boss or pastor, you guide them toward a respectful attitude toward others.

And just as your attitude toward others will be "caught" by your kids, you're the one who teaches your kids how to view themselves. Has your daughter caught you stressing over calories or lamenting your reflection in the mirror? Does your son see you accept and embrace new challenges? Every day, you have the opportunity to show your kids how to approach their strengths and their weaknesses.

Translation: If you mess up in front of your kids, it's okay. The important thing is that you handle your mistakes the way you want your kids to, by taking responsibility and moving on.

There's one area in which our kids will almost definitely pick up our attitudes, in which it's incredibly important to be mindful of what we're modeling, and that's the area of family relationships.

Dads, the way you treat your wife teaches your son about how he should treat women as he gets older, and teaches your daughter about what she should expect from men. Your son is watching you to find out how to be a man, how to approach responsibility and take care of others. And your daughter needs you just as much—a father's relationship with his daughter is invaluable for lending her a sense of security and femininity.

The same is true for moms and their sons and daughters. Moms, you're your daughter's model for femininity. And by the way you treat your son, he learns what to expect from women and how to treat them with respect.

Right now, you're presenting your kids an image of parenting in general—the way you treat your kids is a huge predictor of how they'll treat their kids. Your kids pick up your priorities, goals, and jokes. We all remember the Harry

Chapin song, "Cat's in the Cradle." In that song, the father never seems to have enough time to spend with his son, and is disappointed when his son grows up not seeming to have enough time with him. On a much more tragic level, children who are abused often grow up to abuse their own children. If we want our kids to grow up putting family first, we have to put family first.

Obviously, we have an incredible power and responsibility to help our kids develop right attitudes. But as we're trying to model the attitudes we want to pass on to our kids, how do we model something we don't necessarily feel? You probably want your kids to be compassionate and faithful and patient a greater percentage of the time than you are. Which comes first, attitudes or actions? It's a pretty blurry line, but very often, you can create an attitude in yourself by performing the actions that reflect that attitude. You can become more compassionate—and model compassion—by doing kind and compassionate acts. You can infuse your own spiritual devotion by doing the things you want your kids to do.

So we know we can and should model good life principles for our kids. But how can we be strategic and intentional about it?

A good place to start is by doing an audit to determine which values, attitudes, and practices you want to pass on to your kids. Look back at your lists from Chapter 1. What values do you want your kids to adopt? How do you want them to approach church, work, and family? Think about your priorities in the following areas:

- Spirituality. What kind of spiritual lives do you want your kids to have?

- Family. What kind of femininity do you want to model for your daughter? What goals and attitudes do you want to pass on to your son? How do you want them to treat their kids.

- Work. How do you want your kids to set their priorities when they have families of their own? How do you want them to approach work—as a "chore" or as something to be done with joy? How do you want them to balance work and fun?

Once you've got an idea of what you want to model, it's time to do another audit, this time assessing how you're doing. Do you model church attendance the way you'd like to? Are you showing your kids that life is about more than work, and that they're more important to you than anything else in the world? Are you teaching your daughter to expect care and respect from men, and teaching your son to stand up for what's right?

Modeling is a challenge. Life gets hectic, and it's easy to get so caught up in the day-to-day that we forget to think about what our kids are learning about the day-to-day. If we're willing to check our own attitudes and priorities, we can model for our kids right attitudes and actions. And that puts them—and us—in a position to lead a great life.

PERSONAL REFLECTION:

What percent of your attitudes, values, and beliefs would you say you caught from your parents? Is that a good thing? How do you think you're doing in terms of modeling for your kids?

✓ YOUR TO DO LIST:

This chapter is a tall order. This week, create just one opportunity to model good character for your kids. Build a treehouse with your kids and seek to model perseverance, problem solving, and teamwork. Spend a Saturday at a women's and children's center. Bring your spouse flowers.

FOR FURTHER STUDY:

How to Behave So Your Children Will, Too!
     —by Sal Severe, PhD.

The Encouraging Parent: How to Stop Yelling at Your Kids and Start Teaching Them Confidence, Self-Discipline, and Joy
     —by Rod Wallace Kennedy, PhD.

NOTES

Chapter 2

[1] Nina L Dominy, W. Brad Johnson, Christopher Koch, "Perception of Parental Acceptance in Women with Binge Eating Disorder," *Journal of Psychology* 123 (2000).

[2] "When to Hold Your Tongue," *Psychology Today* 29 (1996): 22.

Chapter 4

[1] Dr. Sylvia Rimm, *Dr. Sylvia Rimm's Smart Parenting* (New York: Three Rivers Press, 1996).

[2] Lawrence E. Shapiro, *An Ounce of Prevention: How Parents Can Stop Childhood Behavioral and Emotional Problems Before They Start* (New York: HarperCollins, 2000).

[3] Nancy Samalin and Catherine Whitney, *Loving Without Spoiling* (New York: Contemporary Books, 2003).

Chapter 5

[1] Larry B. Silver, M.D., *The Misunderstood Child: Understanding and Coping with Your Child's Learning Disabilities* (New York: Random House, 1998).

Chapter 6

[1] David and Claudia Arp, "Partners or Parents?" *Marriage Partnership* 14 (1997): 16.

Chapter 7

[1] Michael K. Meyerhoff, "Superficial Self-Esteem," *Pediatrics for Parents,* 22 (2005): 8.

[2] Javad H. Kashani, Donna V. Mehregany, Wesley D. Allen, Kate Kelly, eds., *Raising Happy Children: A Parent's Guide* (New York: Three Rivers Press, 1998).

Chapter 8

[1] Janet Bodnar, "Let Daddy's Girl Grow Up" *Kiplinger's Personal Finance Magazine* 57 (2003).

[2] Nancy Samalin, *Love and Anger* (New York: Viking, 1991).

[3] "Am I Prudent or Overprotective?" *Today's Parent*, August 1, 1998.

[4] Kevin Leman, *What a Difference a Daddy Makes* (Nashville: Thomas Nelson, 2000).

Chapter 9

[1] Roberta M. Berns, *Child, Family, School, Community* (Orlando, Florida: Harcourt College Publishers, 2001).

[2] Perri Klass, "No More Yelling! The New Golden Rules of Discipline, from a Pediatrician Mom Who's Found Better Ways to Get Her Kids to Behave," *Parenting* XVIII (2004).

[3] Holly Bennett, "The Discipline Difference" *Today's Parent* October 1, 2005: 75.

[4] T. Berry Brazelton and Joshua D. Sparrow, *Discipline: the Brazelton Way* (Cambridge: Perseus Books, 2003), 44.

[5] James Dobson, *The Strong-Willed Child* (Wheaton, Ill: Tyndale House, 1997).

[6] Brazelton and Sparrow, *Discipline*, 73.

[7] Sal Severe, *How to Behave So Your Children Will, Too!* (New York: Viking, 2000).

[8] Severe, *How to Behave*.

[9] \Dobson, *The Strong-Willed Child*.

[10] Severe, *How to Behave*.

Chapter 11

1 Bob Chase, *The New Public School Parent*. New York: Penguin, 2002.

2 \Jonathan Schorr, *Hard Lessons: The Promise of an Inner City Charter School*. New York: Ballantine, 2002.

Chapter 12

1 Michelle Kennedy, *Eating* (New York: Barron's Educational Series, Inc., 2003).

2 Cindy Schweich Handler, "The Importance of Doing Nothing," *Parenting* (1999).

Chapter 13

1 Nancy Samalin, *Love and Anger*, 187-207.

2 Susan Page, *The Eight Essential Traits of Couples Who Thrive* (New York: Dell Trade Paperback, 1994).

3 Adele Faber and Elaine Mazlish, *Siblings without Rivalry: How to Help Your Children Live Together So You Can Live Too* (New York: Norton, 1987).